50 HIKES
IN THE
CATSKILLS

2017

Timothy,

Merry Christmas

Grandmother
&
v. Bill

50 HIKES
IN THE CATSKILLS

FIRST EDITION

Derek Dellinger and
Matthew Cathcart

THE COUNTRYMAN PRESS

A division of W. W. Norton & Company

Independent Publishers Since 1923

*This book is dedicated to everyone who works to maintain
and protect our nation's great wild lands. —D. D.*

*To Kimberly, Jon, and Matt, who taught me that not all
geese fly south for the winter. —M. C.*

Map data provided by The New York State Department
of Environmental Conservation

An Invitation To The Reader
Over time, trails can be rerouted and signs and landmarks can be altered. If you find that changes have
occurred on the routes described in this book, please let us know, so that corrections may be made in future
editions. The author and publisher also welcome other comments and suggestions.
Address all correspondence to:

50 Hikes Editor
The Countryman Press
500 Fifth Avenue
New York, NY 10110

For information about permission to reproduce selections from this book, write to
Permissions, The Countryman Press, 500 Fifth Avenue, New York, NY 10110

For information about special discounts for bulk purchases, please contact W. W. Norton
Special Sales at specialsales@wwnorton.com or 800-233-4830

The Countryman Press
www.countrymanpress.com

A division of W. W. Norton & Company, Inc.
500 Fifth Avenue, New York, NY 10110
www.wwnorton.com

978-1-68268-040-7 (pbk.)

10 9 8 7 6 5 4 3 2 1

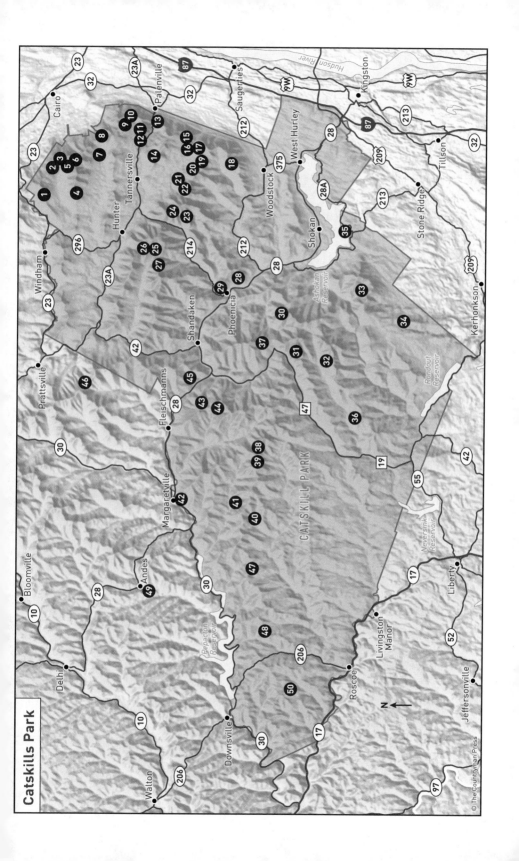

Catskills Park

Contents

III. SOUTHERN | 143

IV. CENTRAL | 173

V. WESTERN | 215

Hikes at a Glance

Hike Name	Region	Distance (miles)	Difficulty
1. Windham High Peak	Northeastern	6.2	Moderate
2. Burnt Knob	Northeastern	2.9	Moderate
3. Acra Point	Northeastern	5.2	Easy
4. Thomas Cole Mountain	Northeastern	5.8	Strenuous
5. Black Dome Mountain	Northeastern	5.2	Strenuous
6. Blackhead Mountain	Northeastern	5	Strenuous
7. Colgate Lake to Dutcher Notch	Northeastern	8.6	Easy
8. Stoppel Point from Stork's Nest Road	Northeastern	8	Strenuous
9. North Point	Northeastern	5.5	Moderate
10. Artist's Rock and Newman's Ledge	Northeastern	2.1	Easy
11. Inspiration Point and Layman's Monument	Northeastern	4.7	Easy
12. Kaaterskill Falls	Northeastern	1	Easy
13. Poet's Ledge	Northeastern	7	Difficult
14. Kaaterskill High Peak from Gillespie Road	Northeastern	6.4	Easy
15. Huckleberry Point	Eastern Central	4.8	Easy
16. Upper Platte Clove Waterfall	Eastern Central	1	Easy
17. Codfish Point from Platte Clove	Eastern Central	4	Easy
18. Overlook Mountain	Eastern Central	4.6	Strenuous
19. Indian Head Mountain Loop	Eastern Central	6.25	Very difficult
20. Twin Mountain	Eastern Central	5.8	Strenuous
21. Dibble's Quarry	Eastern Central	2	Easy
22. Sugarloaf Mountain Loop	Eastern Central	7	Very difficult
23. Plateau Mountain from Warner Creek	Eastern Central	8.5	Strenuous
24. Plateau Mountain from Devil's Tombstone	Eastern Central	6	Strenuous
25. Southwest Hunter Mountain (Leavitt Peak)	Eastern Central	6.2	Difficult
26. Hunter Mountain	Eastern Central	8.2	Strenuous
27. West Kill Mountain	Eastern Central	6.4	Difficult
28. Tremper Mountain	Eastern Central	6.1	Moderate
29. Tanbark Loop	Eastern Central	2.3	Moderate
30. Wittenberg and Cornell Mountains	Southern	9.4	Strenuous
31. Slide Mountain	Southern	6.8	Strenuous

Good for Kids	Camping	Waterfalls	Scenic Views	Notes
	✓		✓	Out and back
✓	✓		✓	Out and back
✓	✓		✓	Loop
			✓	Out and back
			✓	Out and back
	✓		✓	Loop
✓	✓	✓	✓	Out and back
			✓	Out and back
✓	✓		✓	Lollipop
✓	✓		✓	Out and back
✓	✓	✓	✓	Lollipop
✓		✓		Out and back
			✓	Out and back
✓			✓	Out and back
✓				Out and back
✓		✓		Out and back
✓	✓		✓	Out and back
✓			✓	Out and back
	✓		✓	Loop
			✓	Out and back
✓			✓	Out and back
			✓	Loop
			✓	Out and back
	✓		✓	Out and back
	✓	✓	✓	Out and back (bushwhack required)
	✓	✓	✓	Loop
		✓	✓	Out and back
✓	✓		✓	Out and back
✓		✓	✓	Lollipop
	✓		✓	Out and back
✓			✓	Loop

Hike Name	Region	Distance (miles)	Difficulty
32. Table and Peekamoose Mountains	Southern	9	Strenuous
33. Ashokan High Point	Southern	7.5	Moderate
34. Vernooy Kill Falls	Southern	3.4	Easy
35. Ashokan Promenade	Southern	3	Easy
36. Red Hill Fire Tower	Southern	2.8	Easy
37. Giant Ledge and Panther Mountain	Central	6.6	Moderate
38. Graham Mountain	Central	8.3	Moderate
39. Balsam Lake Mountain and Fire Tower	Central	7.5	Moderate
40. Alder Lake Loop	Central	2	Easy
41. Kelly Hollow Loop	Central	3.7	Easy
42. Pakatakan Mountain	Central	3.4	Difficult
43. Belleayre Mountain Ridge	Central	6.3	Strenuous
44. Balsam Mountain	Central	5.2	Moderate
45. Burroughs Memorial/Rochester Hollow	Central	6.1	Moderate
46. Bearpen and Vly Mountains	Central	6.5	Moderate
47. Touch-Me-Not Mountain/Little Pond/Cabot Mountain	Western	7.5	Strenuous
48. Split Rock Lookout	Western	2.4	Moderate
49. Andes Rail Trail and Bullet Hole Spur	Western	3.9	Easy
50. Trout Pond Loop	Western	5.1	Easy

Good for Kids	Camping	Waterfalls	Scenic Views	Notes
	✓		✓	Out and back
	✓		✓	Out and back
✓	✓	✓		Out and back
✓				Out and back
✓			✓	Out and back
	✓		✓	Out and back
			✓	Out and back
	✓		✓	Lollipop
✓	✓			Loop
✓	✓	✓		Loop
			✓	Out and back
	✓		✓	Out and back
	✓		✓	Loop
✓	✓			Lollipop
			✓	Out and back
	✓		✓	Lollipop
✓	✓		✓	Out and back
✓			✓	Lollipop
✓	✓	✓	✓	Loop

Introduction

When I was a sophomore in high school, my father and I were turned on to hiking by a family friend who took us on a short autumn day hike near the Adirondacks. In the splendor of the fall foliage, with the Adirondack high peaks in the distance and endless forest enveloping us, it's no wonder we got hooked: The mountain ranges of New York State offer an altogether different sort of beauty than the western Finger Lakes region, where we lived. Both my dad and I were in pretty good shape—I played soccer and ran track, while my father coached soccer at my high school and played in a couple of local rec leagues. We found the effort of the hike exhilarating, rather than challenging. In retrospect, perhaps, that easy day trip with our friend might have inspired a somewhat overconfident assessment of what a manageable day hike actually looked like. Well, we'd learn soon enough.

Both my father and I were eager to attempt a more serious hike, and soon. Finding the outdoor activities around our home in Syracuse to be "walks" more than "hikes," we had a craving to tackle peaks—even if we didn't quite yet understand what that might entail. From Syracuse, most of the Adirondack region was a four-hour drive away, at least. A drive to the Catskills shaved an hour off that, and given the limited daylight that time of year, the choice was easy. One cold, snowy December weekend, we set out early in the morning and made the drive into the heart of the Catskill Park. Our plan was to hike Giant Ledge, Pan-

ther Mountain, and Slide Mountain—all in one day.

We arrived at the trailhead mid-morning and made our way up the icy trail to Giant Ledge and Panther, the enchanting winter forest scenery capturing our thoughts and steering our conversations. I don't remember too much about the trail itself other than that there was an awful lot more snow on the ground the higher we climbed. Syracuse is of course no slouch when it comes to winter snow accumulation, but I'd never had to fight my way through it like this before. The other details of the hike—the cold, the wind, the difficulty of the trail—all vanished in the intervals between the colorful little trail markers that we followed up the shoulder of the mountain. Eventually we reached Giant Ledge, where we received our first peek at the Catskill landscape, an image that left a profound impression on my adolescent mind. I recall a surge of excitement and awe looking out from that vista, and more than a little trepidation as I realized that we were actually going to attempt to climb Slide, the behemoth jumble of rocky forest commanding our line of sight.

After summiting Panther and returning to the car, we drove up the road to the Slide Mountain parking area and made ready to start the second leg of our hike. At this point it was early afternoon, and most other hikers would soon be heading downhill to return home and warm up. Just before leaving the parking area, distracted by a busy mind already wandering up the trail, I stupidly locked our keys in the car. We had a bulky prepaid cell phone—high technology for the time—so we might have even counted ourselves lucky there … except we were deep in the mountains. There was not a trace of service, of course, so we didn't have much of a choice but to wait for someone to visit the parking area and bail us out. Thankfully, a small group of hikers left the trail shortly after my blunder and offered to drive into town and call a garage for us while we stayed behind at the trailhead. We waited in the cold for over an hour before a tow truck arrived and unlocked our vehicle.

By then it was nearly four o'clock, and the frigid December darkness was already starting to set in. We probably should have taken the incident as a warning, packed up the car, and headed home, content to have enjoyed our previous jaunt through the wilderness. But as my dad and I sat in our idling car, chatting and shivering, waiting for our fingers and toes to warm, it became clear that neither of us was willing to hit the road until we had made it as far up Slide as we could before darkness, wind, cold, hunger, bears, or whatever else might be out there forced us to turn around. Apparently something had affected us on Giant Ledge and Panther, and we were enthralled by these mountains. Or possibly slightly delirious with hypothermia.

Looking back now, I can imagine a number of much less pleasant outcomes to this story. Summiting mountains in the winter is a challenge best undertaken by experienced hikers with the proper equipment and preparations. Summiting mountains in the winter at night is a feat that could very likely lead to a dramatic helicopter rescue for an inexperienced hiker— or, in my case, to becoming inspired

to write a hiking guide with a good friend and fellow mountain enthusiast years later.

That night, my father and I made it all the way to the top of Slide Mountain, almost entirely in the dark. When I think about it now, the recklessness of the idea is almost absurd, but I've never once regretted it. The wind howled through the trees, sending clumps of snow hurling through the air as we trudged up the path to the summit. We were at least somewhat prepared for the circumstances, as it turned out. Shortly after we got onto the trail, my dad pulled an early Christmas present out of his pack: an LED Black Diamond headlamp. As we tromped up the slope, our new headlamps cutting through the endless mountain dark, I don't recall anything from either me or my father other than exhilaration. Even with the lamps, there was little to see but the trail immediately in front of us. When we finally arrived at the summit, it was full night—there were no vistas or viewpoints due to the darkness, and the wind was so brutal that we couldn't spend more than a few minutes on top before turning around. Still, it felt worth it even at the time. We arrived home much later and far more tired than we had expected, but we couldn't wait to recount the trip to friends and family the next day. As if they could have fully understood our excitement … "You call that fun? Sounds like work to me."

My father and I made many trips to the Catskills after that first expedition. We would wake up before sunrise, eat breakfast in the car listening to the Beatles, hike more miles than was perhaps sane to attempt in one day, and drive back home completely exhausted. Over the days that followed each of these excursions, we'd wear our soreness like a badge and begin dreaming of the next adventure. While in recent years, most of my hiking trips have been taken with my wife and friends, my father and I still meet to hike in the Catskills on occasion, and each time our inside jokes and stories of previous hikes are imbued with new life.

I've had the pleasure of enjoying these mountains over the years with people who mean much to me, but regardless of whom you set out with, or whether you wish to explore these trails on your own, the impact of the Catskills is more than just the miles you hike in one day, or the pictures you take from another stunning vista. There is a soul to these mountains that is deeply felt by anyone who visits them. The vitality, beauty, and charm of this place is clear from the peaks to the lowest streams; it pervades the main streets of the mountain towns scattered throughout the Catskills' strange, quiet valleys. There is a feeling of mystery lurking in the cols and cloves, an immediate sense that there is history here—these mountains are low and weathered because they are ancient, after all. These are mountains that have inspired artists and philosophers for countless years, and regardless of whether you approach the Catskills for the adventure or for the simple ambiance, they will doubtless inspire you, too.

There are too many potential destinations in this 700,000-acre park to ever really number all of them, of course, and in the hundreds of hours I have spent in these mountains, I still find myself with that same longing to stay and see more that I felt on that first expedition with my father. Since that day long ago, I have finished the Catskill 3500 Challenge with both my father and my wife. I've explored areas of the park that I never thought I'd visit, and done so in every sort of weather and condition imaginable. Since the Catskills first caused me to fall in love with the mountains, I've hiked all over the country and climbed peaks much taller than the highest Catskill summits, but I've never found another area that feels more like home than this park. Oh, and I still have a hard time pointing the car back toward my house, even after a long, grueling day of miles and miles of wandering within the park boundary.

Wandering the Catskill trails, you'll rarely meet anyone who isn't friendly, cheerful, or grinning from ear to ear. Looking around these ancient forests, it's easy to let that same sense of wonder permeate your own thoughts. I've felt it not only in further exploring the mountains in preparation for this guide, but also by reliving prior trips in putting pen to paper. My hope in writing this guidebook is that you will get as much enjoyment from these mountains as I have over the years. Please appreciate, respect, and protect this wilderness so that others may find the same sense of awe and enchantment for years to come.

—Matthew Cathcart

HISTORY OF THE CATSKILLS

While we may realize consciously that even mountains are not permanent, it is still strange to think just how much the land comprising the vast peaks we know has changed over the ages. The Catskills are relatively young, compared to other mountainous areas in the eastern United States, some of which have been bearing the forces of erosion and shrinking back into the earth for more than 400 million years. The Hudson Valley's most prominent peaks began their existence as a river delta to the west of another, ancient mountain chain: the once-massive Acadian Mountains. Roughly 200 million years ago, as continental drift began to form the Appalachians, the delta region comprising the Catskills was pushed up to create a vast plateau. Individual mountains were not actually distinct at this point, leaving just one massive shelf—surely a sight to behold, though of course there were other drastic differences at the time. The Catskill delta began its existence when its landmass was at the equator, and so this Catskill plateau would have looked quite different in almost every way from the mountains we know today.

Over time, streams began to erode the plateau. Resistant rocks remained, while softer strata washed away. Deep, scenic cloves and valleys were carved out by the whims of erosion. Over millions of years and several ice ages, the Catskill Mountains that we recognize today gradually took shape. Today, the roughly 1,500 square miles of the Catskill Park are home to over a hundred peaks with elevations surpassing 3,000 feet.

In more modern times, an abundance of fish in the pristine mountain streams, plus ample wild game, attracted Lenni-Lenape, Munsee, and several other Native American tribes from the surrounding area. These hunters made annual forays into the mountains, both to hunt and to pass through en route to other destinations, and they created trails that would later be adopted by European settlers (and even turned into hiking paths). However, there is little evidence that Native American tribes ever permanently settled in the Catskills to any significant extent, probably due to the difficulty of farming the rocky mountain soil.

The first Europeans arrived at the Catskills around the early 1600s. Over the next several decades, the Dutch in particular would leave their imprint in place-names, but they generally did not take up permanent residence in the mountains to a significantly greater extent than the Indians had—much better farmland was available in the areas surrounding the Catskills. A large influx of settlers leading to established towns would not occur for some years. What farmsteads there were mostly focused on dairy production, with others turning to wool, maple syrup, apples, and potatoes for their output. Another odd quirk of the Catskills: cauliflower thrives in the mineral-rich soil of the mountains, and it became a profitable export for the region in the early twentieth century.

Despite the initial difficulty of homesteading there, the Catskills soon became a valuable resource for the region, particularly New York City, in ways other than agriculture. The metropolis 90 miles to the south was built in part with bluestone and lumber from the mountains. The first railroads began to thread their way into the Catskills around 1870, radically altering the commerce of the mountains, as well as the sort of New Yorker that this dramatic landscape appealed to. Wealthy residents from the city began to flock to the unique mountain hotels popping up around the eastern escarpment, drawn by the vistas and the clean mountain air. Around this time, the region also became known as a destination for painters, artists, and thinkers, and the hotels and vacationing lifestyle of the period are captured in a number of classic works of art. The Catskill hotels eventually went out of business or burned down, though their foundations remain visible along many of the trails in this guide.

HOW TO PREPARE FOR YOUR HIKE

While it may be tempting to simply drive to the trailhead on a whim, there is a good amount of planning that goes into any successful hike. Preparing for your hike ahead of time may seem tedious, but it should never be overlooked. How well you plan could, in fact, save your life. Listed below is a set of guidelines that should aid you in your journey both on and off the trail.

SAFETY

While exploring the wilderness, your safety and that of your hiking companions should always be your number one concern. To a large extent, backcountry safety involves common sense—stay on the designated trail and be extra cautious when near cliff edges or on slick rocks. However, there are several other things you can do to ensure that your trip remains a safe affair.

- Leave your plans with a friend or family member. Let them know when and where you plan to hike as well as what time you expect to be finished. Establish a cutoff time a few hours after you plan to arrive home, and contact them as soon as you are able to upon returning from the trail. If your safety contact does not hear from you by the cutoff time, this will be a signal that they may need to seek help.
- Familiarize yourself with nearby towns. Look up how far your hike is from the nearest hospital and write down any necessary phone numbers beforehand. It is also a good idea to make note of nearby grocery and convenience stores, as well as gas stations, on the way to your destination.

Spotty cell reception in the mountains can often make looking up this information difficult on the go.

- Bring your cell phone with you on your hike. Many of the trailheads in the Catskills have little to no cell service, but that doesn't mean you shouldn't have your phone on you anyway. You may be able to make a quick phone call or send a message at higher elevations. Additionally, every trail register you will sign contains the contact information for the local park rangers. Save this information to your phone or write it down. It could save your life! Be mindful of your cell phone's battery charge. Reception may come and go, but without a charge, your phone is guaranteed to be useless in the backcountry. Simply carrying a cell phone is not a replacement for ample planning.

WEATHER

The weather in the mountains can change very quickly, fluctuating between extremes of hot and cold, while rain clouds can make precipitation even when the forecast calls for dry conditions. Under normal circumstances, the temperature drops by roughly 3°F for every 1,000 feet of elevation gain. This can be exacerbated even further by the wind, which is often much stronger the higher you climb. Before you embark on your hike, check the weather forecast and plan to the best of your ability, but be aware that the conditions may change without warning. The Catskills are relatively small mountains, but extremes of weather can lead to injury or death in any season. In the event of inclement weather or an unexpected storm starting in the middle of your hike, be prepared to turn around if necessary. Safety should always be your number one concern. The mountains will still be there next time!

ETIQUETTE

The subject of trail etiquette is mostly concerned with preserving the serene quality of the woods for others to enjoy, both immediately and in the future. Do your best to be courteous to those sharing the trails with you. This should be easy to do, since the people you'll meet on the trail will generally be cheerful and friendly. It's not uncommon to strike up amiable conversations with fellow hikers, or to offer a neighborly greeting as you pass. Everyone hikes at a different pace, so let others pass if they wish to go faster, and yield to hikers coming downhill, especially when the trail is steep and narrow. If you are hiking in a group, try to keep your noise level low so that others may enjoy the peacefulness of the forest. Stay on the trail to minimize erosion and preserve the delicate flora that inhabits the mountains. Lastly, follow Leave No Trace principles and pack out anything you pack in. If you have the pack space, carry out any trash that may have been left behind by others. It is the responsibility of everyone to ensure that the wilderness remains pristine for future generations to enjoy.

WINTER

Hiking in the winter can be an exciting undertaking. The cold air feels clean and refreshing, the lack of foliage on the trees can uncover previously hidden vistas, and the frigid landscape breathes an exciting new life into areas you may have previously visited. That being said, the risks associated with hiking are augmented and intensified during the winter months. For this reason, winter hiking should only be attempted by experienced hikers. Weather, snow, ice,

and hypothermia are very real dangers that can be fatal if you are not very well prepared, especially when combined with the magnifying effect that elevation gain has on these variables. The weather conditions, snow accumulation, and icy buildup are often much more drastic at elevation than at the parking area. It is imperative to plan ahead extensively if you are going to attempt hiking in the winter. No one wants to bail before they reach their desired destination, but you may need to turn around halfway through your hike even if you do come prepared. It can be difficult to make this call, but it is far better to be safe than to risk serious injury or death. Use common sense and be cautious.

Wintertime hiking often requires the use of additional equipment both for ease of hiking and for safety on the trail. Snowshoes and poles should be used when snowy conditions are present, and crampons or traction devices will help to provide steady footing in slippery areas. Be sure to bring hats, gloves, and extra layers of clothing. Additional items such as gaiters, hand warmers, and a thermos of hot chocolate or coffee can make your hike more comfortable and enjoyable. Keep in mind, however, that this extra gear is a supplement and should not be a replacement for planning ahead.

WHAT TO BRING ON YOUR HIKE

Ask any number of hikers what they bring on a hike and you will likely get a variety of answers, ranging from the practical to the extravagant and everywhere in between. Some people embrace the ultralight ideology, bringing only essential lightweight items that often serve dual purposes, while other prefer to carry a little bit of extra weight for the sake of comfort and security. Whatever your style may be, there are a few things that just about everyone can agree on.

BACKPACK

A comfortable backpack is a must for any hike longer than a mile or two. Just about any pack will do as long as you find it agreeable. While not imperative, packs with hip or chest belts can increase load stability and greatly improve your balance on the trail. Other popular features include multiple pockets or compartments and hydration reservoirs. Whichever backpack you choose, make sure everything you plan on bringing will comfortably fit inside before you leave for the trailhead.

HIKING BOOTS

The type of hiking boots you should wear is largely a matter of preference, but it is beneficial to know what options exist so you can make the choice that will suit you best. High-top hiking boots offer the most ankle support and are quite durable, but are much more expensive. Low-cut boots and trail-running shoes let feet breathe more easily, allow a greater range of motion, and are usually cheaper. A variety of different rubber soles are available, with varying levels of stickiness and durability—perhaps the most important aspect to consider, given that many of the trails are very rocky and uneven. Waterproof or treated boots can help make your feet more comfortable as well. Whatever type of shoes you choose, be sure to break them in beforehand. Waiting until the day of your hike to break in your shoes will likely result in uncomfortable, hot, blistery feet.

WATER

You will want to bring about a liter of water for every 2–3 miles you plan to hike. However, this amount is just a guideline, and you will need to carry more water during hot summer months. There is an abundance of water in the Catskills, and refilling your water bottle or hydration bladder from a mountain spring or stream midhike is a rewarding, refreshing experience. This technique can greatly reduce the amount of water you need to carry at any given time, but be aware that many springs only run seasonally. Additionally, all water should be treated before drinking to remove or kill harmful bacteria and protozoa such as Giardia, E. coli, and Salmonella. A number of options exist, including chemical treatments, filtration systems, or simply boiling water beforehand. Chemical treatments such as iodine or chlorine dioxide tablets are cheap and lightweight, but they need to work for a minimum of half an hour before the water is safe to drink, and they can leave a foul aftertaste. Backcountry water filters are more expensive, bulkier, and heavier, but they deliver immediate results without any impact on the flavor of the water.

FOOD

In general you will want to bring 2–3 pounds of food per person per day of hiking. As with water, this value is a guideline. You may need to bring more or less food depending on how strenuous your route is as well as your metabolism. It is a good idea to bring a little more than you think you'll need if you are unsure—it is better to carry extra food back to your car than it is to run out of food halfway through your hike. Energy and granola bars, dried fruit and nuts, candy bars, and jerky are excellent, highly portable choices that will provide your body with the necessary protein, carbohydrates, and electrolytes it needs to keep you energized and on the trail.

CLOTHING

It is important to stay prepared for any sudden weather changes by bringing along extra layers of clothing. Windy, exposed summits may require you to add layers of clothing to stay warm, while the exertion of the climb up to these summits will cause you to remove layers to keep cool. The key to staying comfortable is planning for a wide variety of conditions. Choose clothing that is versatile. Wool or synthetic blends insulate well and also breathe, letting moisture evaporate quickly, so that your body can regulate its temperature more naturally. Cotton clothing traps moisture and insulates poorly when wet. For this reason, you should try to avoid cotton clothing as much as possible.

It is a good idea, even in warmer weather, to always bring a long-sleeved shirt or jacket with you. A windbreaker can extend your visit to a blustery vista, and a rain jacket or poncho will further protect you from less-than-pleasant weather conditions. Bring a hat and gloves if the weather will be chilly, since your hands and head radiate a significant amount of heat. Lastly, it's always a good idea to bring an extra pair of socks in case your feet become wet.

FIRST AID KIT

Your first aid kit does not need to be extensive, but a few basic items will help alleviate any minor injuries you may sustain on your hike. You can create your own first aid kit out of things commonly found at a drugstore, such as adhesive bandages, gauze, medical tape, alcohol swabs, hand sanitizer, antibiotic ointment, tweezers, moleskin (or other blister-relief material), and over-the-counter pain medication. If you are taking any prescription medication, be sure to pack any doses you would normally take throughout the day as well.

All of these items easily fit inside a plastic bag and will help ensure your safety on the trail.

FLASHLIGHT/HEADLAMP

It is always wise to bring a headlamp or lightweight flashlight along on your hike, even if you're planning on finishing well before dusk. You never know when an abrupt change in conditions (or an innocent error reading the trail map) may delay your return to your car by several hours. In spring, fall, and winter, nightfall can sneak up on you. If you are forced to make your return to the trailhead in the dark, don't panic. Simply pay close attention to the trail, and take extra time to orient yourself at each intersection. Most trail markers are reflective and thus easy to follow even at night, provided you have a good source of light.

OTHER NONESSENTIAL ITEMS

To make your hike even more satisfying, you may wish to bring along some items solely for your own enjoyment. Typical nonessential items you will find in hikers' packs include binoculars, a camera, seat pads or packable chairs, small musical instruments such as harmonicas, a notebook and pen or pencil, and a hip flask.

BEAR SAFETY

Black bears play a vital part in New York's ecosystem, and when you are hiking and camping, it is important to remember that you are sharing their home with them—you are the visitor, not them. Most animals want a confrontation even less than you do. Always respect the wild creatures that call the mountains their home, and protect yourself (and the bears) by taking basic precautions. Most rules of bear safety boil down to an essential principle: Do nothing that will unnecessarily attract the attention of bears in the first place. For this reason, you must always be careful when camping and hiking to not feed these intelligent and potentially dangerous animals.

Black bears are omnivorous, and in the wild they live off of fruit, nuts, seeds, insects, grasses, and carrion. Plant foods can make up as much as 90 percent of a bear's diet. It is important to realize that bears, while powerful and imposing creatures, are nonetheless scavengers much more than they are hunters. Most of their day is spent searching for sustenance. Thus, any food made available to them by lazy or unmindful humans will be happily set upon and consumed. Bears are intelligent animals that learn from past experiences. If searching a certain location or repeating a certain activity results in food, a bear will attempt to recreate this scenario again in the future. Thus, food left out around a camp, in close proximity to humans, becomes dangerous for both the bear and the humans. Likewise, if a bear encounters a human and does not acquire any food as a result of the encounter, the bear will have no reason to seek out humans again in the future.

To be clear, the chances of a deadly encounter with a black bear in New York State are extremely low. In the past century, there has been only one recorded human death by bear in the region. If you do spot a bear nearby, do not run. Back away slowly, speaking in a low, calm voice to ensure that the bear recognizes you as a human and not a prey animal. Hiking in a group is usually a deterrent on its own, but if you are alone, attempt to make yourself look as large as possible by raising your arms and taking to high ground while continuing to make noise. Make sure the bear has a clear route to flee the encounter—a bear that feels trapped is likely to behave more aggressively. Do not scream or shriek. If the bear stands up on its hind legs, it is most likely just trying to get a better sense of the situation, not issuing a threat. While black bear encounters tend not to be as deadly as encounters with brown bears or grizzlies out west, the recommended strategy in the unlikely event of an attack is much different. If a black bear does attack you, do not play dead: Always fight back.

The Catskill Mountains are home to about 30–35 percent of the black bears in New York State, and while this is a significant population, it by no means should suggest that you will run into bears on a regular basis. The authors of this guide have spent, combined, hundreds of hours hiking in the Catskill Mountains, and between them they have only seen bears near the trail on two occasions. Fear of a bear encounter is no reason to stay home and miss out on the backwoods charm of the mountains.

LYME DISEASE

Bears may be the most dramatic danger in the backwoods, but a far more likely risk comes in a much smaller form. Ticks are a rapidly growing problem in the northeastern United States, and an encounter with one is more likely to endanger your health than a run-in with a skittish black bear. In the United States, about 300,000 infections occur each year. The northeast is unfortunately a hotbed for Lyme disease, with a vast majority of all cases in the United States occurring in these states.

Lyme disease is spread by an infected tick—not every tick bite will result in Lyme disease. Of course, the tick has to bite you before it can transmit the disease, so the best way to avoid Lyme is to catch any ticks while they're still crawling on you. If you do contract Lyme, the disease may produce a rash, flu-like symptoms, and pain in joints within a few weeks. The most obvious indication that you have Lyme is the notorious "bull's-eye" rash, though not everyone develops this rash. Without the rash, the symptoms of Lyme can be difficult to distinguish from mono or simply a stubborn flu, so if you think you may have contracted Lyme, it is always best to play it safe and get tested. Untreated, it will eventually result in chronic arthritis and nervous system disorders.

Check yourself regularly while hiking, and especially afterward. Deer ticks are very small and can be easy to miss. Tuck your pants into your socks and boots, and apply insect repellent containing DEET. Wearing light-colored clothing will make it somewhat easier to see any unwanted passengers crawling on you. Finally, showering and changing clothes immediately following your hike is the best way to check yourself for parasites.

NOTABLE TOWNS OF THE CATSKILLS

PALENVILLE

For many of the hikes in this guide, the hamlet of Palenville will be your gateway into the mountains—nestled at the foot of the Catskills along the route most commonly taken into the northern section of the park. While the town is small, and lacks the central Main Street shopping district of other Catskill towns, there are still a number of options for a pit stop on your way to or from a hike. Circle W Market, the modern-rustic deli near the western end of town, is the perfect place to stop for breakfast on your

way into the mountains—and to stock up on snacks for the trail. More restaurants, bars, and lodging options can be found along NY-32A, as Palenville extends along this route south.

TANNERSVILLE

As Palenville serves as the gateway to the northern section of the Catskills, Tannersville is perhaps the heart of it. With a long, busy Main Street, Tannersville offers more options for food and drink than perhaps any other town in the interior of the park. A small café called Twin Peaks perfectly captures the atmosphere of a folksy, rustic coffee shop (and, fortunately, without the creepy unease of its television namesake), but perhaps even more appealing than the coffee are the made-to-order doughnuts that come in a variety of flavors. Melt-in-your-mouth fresh, these doughnuts are not to be missed. Just down the street, Last Chance Antiques & Cheese Café is as esoteric as the name suggests, with a large beer selection and solid pub-style food offerings, too. For those looking for a quick, classic meal, Mama's Boy Burgers hits the spot, especially after a day of hiking. Their ice cream offerings are a perfect compliment to their local, grass-fed burgers.

Of course, as the Catskills' busiest tourist town, Tannersville offers much more still, with a variety of restaurants and cafés covering the culinary spectrum, a winery, a performing arts center, antique shops, and perhaps most importantly, a scenic Main Street backed by mountains, ideal for a late afternoon of strolling. Nearby are a number of hotels and bed-and-breakfasts should you wish to stay the night (but not in a tent). Like the mountains that surround it, Tannersville is a charming, timeless destination that is not to be missed.

WOODSTOCK

Perhaps the most overtly touristy destination in the Catskills, and certainly the most enthusiastic about its hippie roots, Woodstock actually had little to do with the famous music festival that shared its name. The festival was named Woodstock after the investment group that funded the concert—Woodstock Ventures—but took place on a dairy farm in Bethel, in Sullivan County, more than 40 miles southwest of the town of Woodstock. Of course, the town is still famous as a home for arts and culture, and maintains a vibrant, eclectic music scene. Tinker Street and Mill Hill Road serve as the town's main drag, with dozens of businesses and several small parks adding up to an easily walkable, scenic shopping district.

Bread Alone is the place to go if you're in the mood for coffee or pastries (or, of course, a fresh loaf of bread), and nearby Catskill Mountain Pizza is a great choice for a delicious posthike meal on a budget. Woodstock and Bearsville are home to a wide array of sit-down restaurants as well, from the casual to the upscale. In addition to dining, the town offers everything from books to boutiques. With Overlook Mountain rising to the north of town, Woodstock truly is a lovely destination on its own, and you'll find plenty of offerings for food, drink, shopping, and entertainment—something to cater to almost every taste, but especially those with a fondness for tie-dye.

PHOENICIA

Miles from the interstate, deep in the interior of the park—at almost its exact center, in fact—Phoenicia has a curious backwoods charm. With only a few hundred inhabitants, it is a thriving tourist town located about as far from tourists as you can get. Phoenicia secured its status in the region by railway, originally—when the Ulster and Delaware Railroad serving the Catskills landed at Phoenicia as one of its first stops, the town quickly adapted to accommodate the influx of visitors. In the modern era, a handful of nearby ski resorts have helped Phoenicia to retain its status as the destination town in the central Catskills region. This popularity has been further secured by a compact Main Street offering plenty to do, just off the scenic Esopus Creek.

While significantly smaller than nearby Woodstock, Phoenicia offers a similar mix of dining and shopping to appeal to day-trippers and locals alike. A few blocks from the town center, the Empire State Railway Museum educates visitors on the history and significance of the region's railroads. Just outside of town, the busy Phoenicia Diner offers a more upscale, locally focused take on traditional comfort food, and is often packed on weekends with travelers from all over the region.

SHOKAN

Just north of the Ashokan Reservoir, the hamlet of Shokan is barely large enough to register as a town when you're driving through: It appears more like a collection of roadside businesses. But on your way into or out of the central Catskills, Shokan makes for a nice, low-key roadside visit, especially if you aren't in the mood for a more crowded destination like Phoenicia. Olive's Country Store and Café sells a variety of snacks and groceries, along with an eclectic mix of touristy gifts—think lots of bear statues and wood carvings. Down the street, Winchell's Pizza & BBQ is a homey, quiet spot for filling grub, with a friendly owner whose passion is unmistakable.

I.

NORTHEASTERN

Windham High Peak

Windham High Peak is the most northerly 3,500-foot peak in the Catskill Mountains, with views over the Schoharie and Mohawk Valleys to Albany. Though lacking the elevation of many of its peers in the range, Windham nonetheless offers excellent views from several vistas as well as beautiful passages through old-growth forest. For more ambitious hikers, the route can be extended to include Burnt Knob and its vistas (an additional 3.5 miles).

DISTANCE: 6.2 miles

TYPE: Out and back

TOTAL ELEVATION GAIN: 1,480 feet

MAXIMUM ELEVATION: 3,525 feet

DIFFICULTY: Moderate

HIKING TIME: 3.5 hours

GETTING THERE

Take Exit 20 (Saugerties) from the New York State Thruway, then turn left onto NY-212/NY-32. At the traffic light, take a right onto NY-32 North. In 6 miles, continue straight onto NY-32A. In 1.9 miles, turn left onto Route 23A, and drive up the winding mountain road toward Tannersville. After driving through Tannersville, turn right at the traffic light onto Hill Street (County Route 23C). Follow NY-23C for 6.1 miles, then turn right onto Maplecrest Road (NY-40). Continue on Maplecrest Road for 1.9 miles, then turn right onto Big Hollow Road. In 1.8 miles, turn left onto Peck Road, and follow it until you arrive at the parking area.

GPS SHORTCUT

Type "Peck Road, Maplecrest, NY" into Google Maps and your GPS will lead you to the start of Peck Road. The parking area is at the end of the road.

THE TRAIL

Head north following the yellow blazes on an old woods road. The trail is fre-

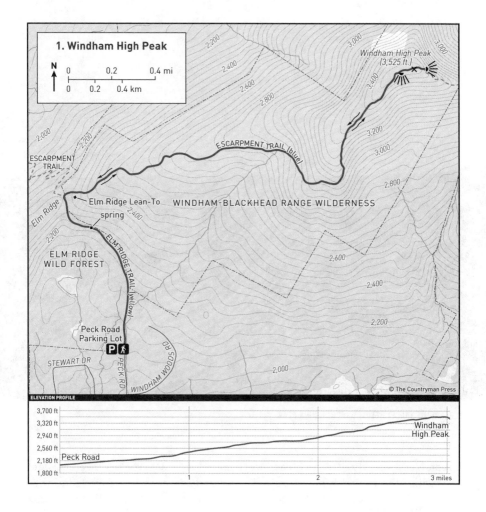

1. Windham High Peak

N

| 0 | 0.2 | 0.4 mi |
| 0 | 0.2 | 0.4 km |

Windham High Peak
(3,525 ft.)

ESCARPMENT TRAIL (blue)

ESCARPMENT
TRAIL

Elm Ridge Lean-To   WINDHAM-BLACKHEAD RANGE WILDERNESS

Elm Ridge
spring

ELM RIDGE
WILD FOREST

ELM RIDGE TRAIL (yellow)

Peck Road
Parking Lot

P

STEWART DR

PECK RD.

WINDHAM WOODS RD

© The Countryman Press

ELEVATION PROFILE

| 3,700 ft |
| 3,320 ft |
| 2,940 ft |
| 2,560 ft |
| 2,180 ft |
| 1,800 ft |

Windham
High Peak

Peck Road

1   2   3 miles

quently muddy throughout the year, though short bypass trails have been built around some of the wettest sections. In a little more than half a mile, you will pass a spring, after which the trail will begin to climb.

Soon, you will arrive at a junction with the blue-blazed Escarpment Trail. Turn right onto the Escarpment Trail. Shortly after, look to your right to catch a glimpse of the Elm Ridge Lean-To through the trees. Continue to follow the blue blazes as the trail begins to ascend more steeply. As you climb, you

will enter a dense forest of old-growth Norway spruce, one of the few remaining in the Catskills.

Eventually you will begin to find views through the trees, looking over your shoulder toward the Blackhead Range. About 2.5 miles into the hike, the trail bears to the left and begins an even steeper climb.

Just under 3 miles in, a side trail to the right of the path leads to the first major viewpoint. With excellent views looking1 out over the Blackhead Range, this is an ideal spot to stop for

BLACK DOME VALLEY BELOW WINDHAM HIGH PEAK

a rest. Very shortly after is a second viewpoint, though with more limited views.

Just after the 3-mile mark, you will reach the summit of Windham High Peak, indicated by a USGS marker embedded in a rock. Only 200 feet beyond the peak is a rock ledge with views of the Hudson Valley and, on a clear day, north to Albany.

When you are ready to descend, retrace your steps to your car.

Burnt Knob

2

DISTANCE: 2.9 miles

TYPE: Out and back

TOTAL ELEVATION GAIN: 1,030 feet

MAXIMUM ELEVATION: 3,180 feet

DIFFICULTY: Moderate

HIKING TIME: 2 hours

Located along the Escarpment Trail, Burnt Knob rewards hikers with panoramic views of the Blackhead Range. The vista isn't terribly far from one of the more popular parking areas in the Catskill Park, but it is rarely a destination point, due to the plethora of views scattered throughout the surrounding wilderness. The described route makes for a great day trip, with plenty of options to lengthen your hike if you're feeling adventurous.

GETTING THERE

Take Exit 20 (Saugerties) from the New York State Thruway, then turn left onto NY-212/NY-32. At the traffic light, take a right onto NY-32 North. In 6 miles, continue straight onto NY-32A. In 1.9 miles, turn left onto Route 23A, and drive up the winding mountain road toward Tannersville. After driving through Tannersville, turn right at the traffic light onto Hill Street (County Route 23C). Head north on NY-23C for 6.1 miles. Turn right onto County Route 40, and follow it until you come to the small town of Maplecrest, in about 2 miles. Veer right onto Big Hollow Road and drive for 4 miles. The parking area is at the very end of the road. Be aware that the last mile or so of this road is considered seasonal and is not maintained during winter months. During times of heavy snowfall, you may need to park on the side of the road, as the parking area is rarely plowed.

GPS SHORTCUT

Type "Acra Point" into Google Maps and your GPS will navigate you to the appropriate trailhead. The Acra Point hike on page 32 also begins from this trailhead.

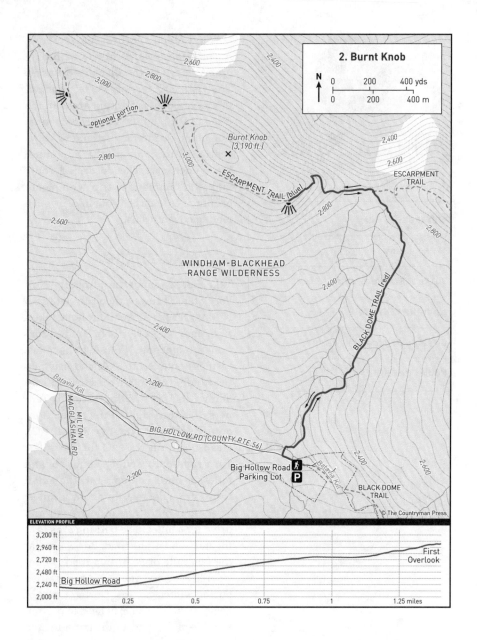

THE TRAIL

Walk up Big Hollow Road toward Maplecrest. The trailhead is slightly before the parking area on the right side of the road. Pick up the Black Dome Trail and follow the red blazes into the woods, crossing the Batavia Kill on a footbridge.

The path will lead you to yet another water crossing shortly thereafter. This crossing lacks a footbridge, and in periods of high runoff or in very wet seasons, it may be impossible to cross without getting wet. Pick your way across the run and continue following the blazes. For the next half mile the trail follows the stream uphill, occasionally cross-ing small seasonal tributaries and runs feeding into the main flow. Eventually, you will start to veer left, leaving the stream behind.

The forest here is mostly hemlock, spruce, and various hardwoods. Look out through the trees when you stop to take a break, as you'll be able to catch obscured views of the Blackhead Range in the distance to the south. You'll have a wide panoramic view of the range at the vista, but these little glimpses will whet your appetite and keep you going when you're out of breath. The grade is relatively steady for the entire ascent.

After 1.1 miles, the Black Dome Trail ends at the junction of the Escarpment Trail. Turning right here will take you to Acra Point, another fantastic vista, in just 0.7 mile. But to stick to this route, turn left here and follow the blue blazes for 0.35 mile. There is a short steep climb in about a tenth of a mile, but the trail levels sig-nificantly afterward. The viewpoint will be on the left, boasting wide-open views of the entire Blackhead Range and the valley below. The viewing area is broad and flat, with enough room for several people to comfortably break, making it a great place to sit back and have a snack.

When you are finished taking in the view, rejoin the Escarpment Trail and return the way you came, descending via the Black Dome Trail. Alternatively, you could continue heading northwest for 1 mile on the blue-blazed Escarp-ment Trail. This will take you to two additional viewpoints. The first is on the right side of the trail, facing north about 0.5 miles from Burnt Knob, and the second is to the left side of the trail, a mile from Burnt Knob. From the second of these vistas, you can see Thomas Cole Mountain and Camel's Hump to the left and Windham High Peak towering to the right. The trail to these viewpoints largely follows the ridgeline. There are a few rolling hills, but otherwise there isn't a great deal of fluctuation in elevation. Including this section of trail on your hike will add 2 miles to your trip, for a total of 4.9 miles overall. Return to your vehicle the same way you came.

BLACKHEAD AND BLACK DOME AS SEEN FROM BURNT KNOB

Acra Point

DISTANCE: 5.2 miles

TYPE: Loop

TOTAL ELEVATION GAIN: 860 feet

MAXIMUM ELEVATION: 3,105 feet

DIFFICULTY: Easy

HIKING TIME: 3 hours

Attracting hikers with a variety of geographical highlights, the Acra Point loop offers commanding views of the Hudson Valley and the surrounding countryside, in addition to one of the best vistas facing the Blackhead Range. The well-travelled trails are easy to navigate, and the serene 2-mile stretch of the Escarpment Trail south of the peak leads through densely wooded, ancient-feeling forest.

GETTING THERE

Take Exit 20 (Saugerties) from the New York State Thruway, then turn left onto NY-212/NY-32. At the traffic light, take a right onto NY-32 North. In 6 miles, continue straight onto NY-32A. In 1.9 miles, turn left onto Route 23A, and drive up the winding mountain road toward Tannersville. After driving through Tannersville, turn right at the traffic light onto Hill Street (County Route 23C). Head north on NY-23C for 6.1 miles. Turn right onto County Route 40, and follow it until you come to the small town of Maplecrest, about 2 miles farther. Veer right onto Big Hollow Road and drive for 4 miles. The parking area is at the very end of the road. Be aware that the last mile or so of this road is considered seasonal and is not maintained during winter months. During times of heavy snowfall, you may need to park on the side of the road, as the parking area is rarely plowed.

GPS SHORTCUT

Type "Acra Point" into Google Maps and your GPS will navigate you to the appropriate trailhead. The Burnt Knob hike on page 29 also begins from this trailhead.

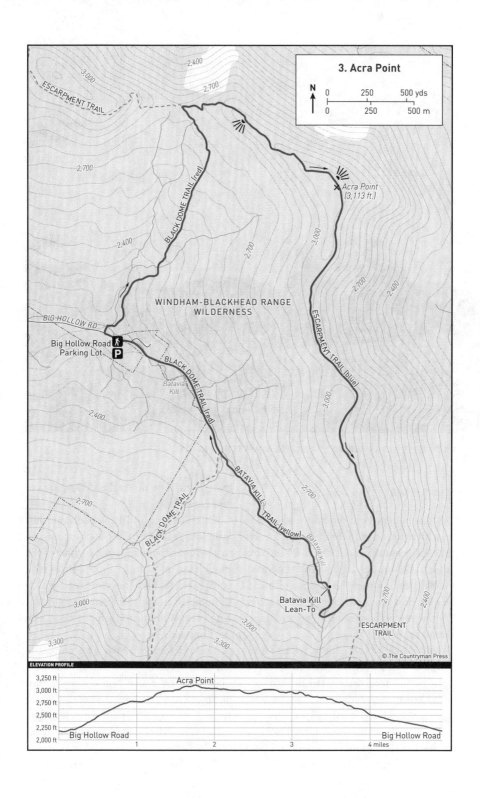

3. Acra Point

N

| 0 | 250 | 500 yds |
| 0 | 250 | 500 m |

ESCARPMENT TRAIL

BLACK DOME TRAIL (red)

2,400

2,700

3,000

2,700

2,400

✕ Acra Point
(3,113 ft.)

2,700

3,000

2,700

2,400

WINDHAM-BLACKHEAD RANGE WILDERNESS

BIG HOLLOW RD

ESCARPMENT TRAIL (blue)

Big Hollow Road Parking Lot

BLACK DOME TRAIL (red)

Batavia Kill

3,000

2,400

2,700

BATAVIA KILL TRAIL (yellow)

Batavia Kill

2,700

BLACK DOME TRAIL

3,000

3,000

Batavia Kill Lean-To

2,400

2,700

ESCARPMENT TRAIL

3,300

3,300

3,300

© The Countryman Press

ELEVATION PROFILE

3,250 ft	Acra Point
3,000 ft	
2,750 ft	
2,500 ft	
2,250 ft	
2,000 ft	Big Hollow Road

1   2   3   Big Hollow Road   4 miles

HIKERS ENJOY THE VIEW TOWARD THE BLACKHEAD RANGE FROM ACRA POINT

THE TRAIL

On foot, retrace your path down the road on which you arrived for a short distance to reach the trailhead for Acra Point. You will spot a wooden bridge and the Batavia Kill creek. Cross the bridge, followed by a second creek crossing shortly after. Follow the red blazes uphill on the Black Dome Trail.

With Blackhead, Black Dome, and Thomas Cole behind you, hike for 1 mile as the trail winds through hardwood and spruce forest. At the first trail junction, head right toward Acra Point, now following the aqua-green blazes of the Escarpment Trail and the Long Path, a 357-mile long-distance hiking trail that winds throughout New Jersey and New York.

Climb a small hill to reach another junction. A left turn here will bring you to a ledge with an impressive view of the Blackhead Mountain Range—the side trail is short, and the view well worth it. Looking northwest from here, Burnt Knob and Windham High Peak can also be glimpsed.

Soon after, you will approach the summit of Acra Point, though the best views, to the south and the west, can be found at the lookout shortly before Acra Point itself. From a rock ledge, enjoy views of the countryside sprawling out below.

Take the Escarpment Trail along a

wide ridge with high ledges. Continue for another 1.75 miles. At this intersection, the Escarpment Trail continues up over Blackhead Mountain—a challenging, steep hike—while the Batavia Kill Trail returns to the DEC parking lot. Turn right onto the yellow-blazed Batavia Kill Trail.

Shortly after, you will pass the Batavia Kill Lean-To. Continue until the trail ends at another junction, where a left turn will again send you toward a steep ascent, this time of Black Dome Mountain. Veer to the right and follow the red blazes along the side of Batavia Kill creek for another half mile to return to your car.

LOOKING WEST TOWARD BURNT KNOB FROM ACRA POINT

Thomas Cole Mountain

DISTANCE: 5.8 miles

TYPE: Out and back

TOTAL ELEVATION GAIN: 1,840 feet

MAXIMUM ELEVATION: 3,940 feet

DIFFICULTY: Strenuous

HIKING TIME: 4 hours

Named after the renowned eighteenth-century artist who painted several Catskill landscapes, Thomas Cole Mountain is nestled next to Black Dome Mountain in the Windham Blackhead Wilderness. While not unpopular by any stretch, Thomas Cole is probably the quietest high peak in the range, especially when approaching from the west. The route described here will take you on a lightly travelled footpath that traverses Caudal and Camel's Hump as well, two of the smaller summits that share residency in the Blackhead Range.

GETTING THERE

Take Exit 20 (Saugerties) from the New York State Thruway, then turn left onto NY-212/NY-32. At the traffic light, take a right onto NY-32 North. In 6 miles, continue straight onto NY-32A. In 1.9 miles, turn left onto Route 23A, and drive up the winding mountain road toward Tannersville. After driving through Tannersville, turn right at the traffic light onto Hill Street (County Route 23C). Head north on NY-23C for 6.1 miles. Turn right onto County Route 40, and follow it for 1 mile before turning right onto Hauser Road. Follow Hauser Road until it ends, and turn right again onto Elmer Barnum Road, continuing on about half a mile. The parking area is a wide turnaround at the end of the road.

GPS SHORTCUT

Search Google Maps for "Hauser Road & Barnum Road" and follow your GPS to the intersection. Follow Elmer Barnum Road to where it ends to reach the trailhead.

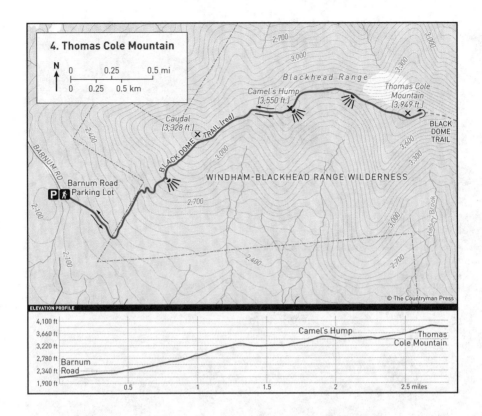

4. Thomas Cole Mountain

N

0   0.25   0.5 mi
0   0.25   0.5 km

Blackhead Range

Thomas Cole Mountain (3,949 ft.)

Camel's Hump (3,550 ft.)

Caudal (3,328 ft.)

BLACK DOME TRAIL (red)

BARNUM RD.

Barnum Road Parking Lot

P

WINDHAM-BLACKHEAD RANGE WILDERNESS

BLACK DOME TRAIL

Halsey Brook

© The Countryman Press

ELEVATION PROFILE

4,100 ft
3,660 ft
3,220 ft
2,780 ft
2,340 ft
1,900 ft

Barnum Road

Camel's Hump

Thomas Cole Mountain

0.5   1   1.5   2   2.5 miles

THE TRAIL

Follow a rocky jeep road from the parking area, heading into the woods on the Black Dome Trail, a red-blazed path that spans nearly the entire Blackhead Range. You will follow the red trail markers for the entirety of the hike. The first portion of the trail crosses private land, so please stay on the designated path and respect the landowner's wishes. After nearly half a mile you will come to a DEC register and turn left to start climbing uphill. The trail ascends moderately through pleasant open forest along a nicely maintained trail for 0.4 mile before twisting to the right. At this point you will begin climbing much more aggressively by way of a few switchbacks that will lead you through several steep sections that are occasionally scattered with boulders. After switchbacking through these rocky segments, the trail begins ascending more directly. There is a nice viewpoint that faces southeast about halfway up Caudal, the first hill you will climb today.

The crest of Caudal is roughly 0.3 mile from the viewpoint and is a small round area sparsely covered with trees and underbrush. Once you reach the top, the trail will begin descending immediately, dropping about 150 feet before leveling for nearly 0.3 mile. Your next climb will be up Camel's Hump, which ascends roughly 350 feet in just over a quarter of a mile. The trail here is very direct and very steep, so take your time. Once you reach the top there is another vista to the right, which also faces southeast.

ASCENDING THE TRAIL TO THOMAS COLE

VIEW OF THOMAS COLE AND CAMEL'S HUMP FROM WINDHAM HIGH PEAK

Continue on the Black Dome Trail, descending into the col between Camel's Hump and Thomas Cole. The trail here is easy and enjoyable, as it follows the ridgeline through scraggly evergreen trees lacing the rocky terrain. You may be able to look out into the valley below, but most of the views are obscured by trees. A little less than half a mile from Camel's Hump, you will begin to ascend sharply once more as you begin to climb up the shoulder of Thomas Cole. The conifer forest becomes much more dense here, and you will notice a good amount of blowdown off-trail. Continue climbing and reach the summit of Thomas Cole Mountain in about 0.5 mile. The trail will begin to level out as you come to the peak. There are no views from the top due to the abundance of trees here, mostly spruce and fir, but an open area located on the summit offers hikers a nice place to take a quiet break.

When you are ready, return the way you came, retracing your steps along the red trail back to your vehicle.

Black Dome Mountain

DISTANCE: 5.2 miles

TYPE: Out and back

TOTAL ELEVATION GAIN: 1,830 feet

MAXIMUM ELEVATION: 3,980 feet

DIFFICULTY: Strenuous

HIKING TIME: 4 hours

Flanked on either side by its smaller brothers, Black Dome Mountain is the tallest peak in the Blackhead Range, rising 40 feet above Blackhead Mountain and Thomas Cole Mountain. The peak is the third tallest in the Catskill Park (surpassed by Slide and Hunter), and on a clear day, it rewards hikers with views of Kaaterskill High Peak and Devil's Path further south. The dense populations of fir and spruce trees that inhabit the summit give this mountain its name and add a bit of intrigue to an already appealing hike.

GETTING THERE

Take Exit 20 (Saugerties) from the New York State Thruway, then turn left onto NY-212/NY-32. At the traffic light, take a right onto NY-32 North. In 6 miles, continue straight onto NY-32A. In 1.9 miles, turn left onto Route 23A, and drive up the winding mountain road toward Tannersville. After driving through Tannersville, turn right at the traffic light onto Hill Street (County Route 23C). Head north on NY-23C for 6.1 miles. Turn right onto County Route 40, and follow it until you come to the small town of Maplecrest, about 2 miles. Veer right onto Big Hollow Road and drive for 4 miles. The parking area is at the very end of the road. Be aware that the last mile or so of this road is considered seasonal and is not maintained during winter months. During times of heavy snowfall, you may need to park on the side of the road, as the parking area is rarely plowed.

GPS SHORTCUT

Type "Blackhead Mountain, Jewett, NY" into Google Maps and your GPS will navigate you to the appropriate trailhead.

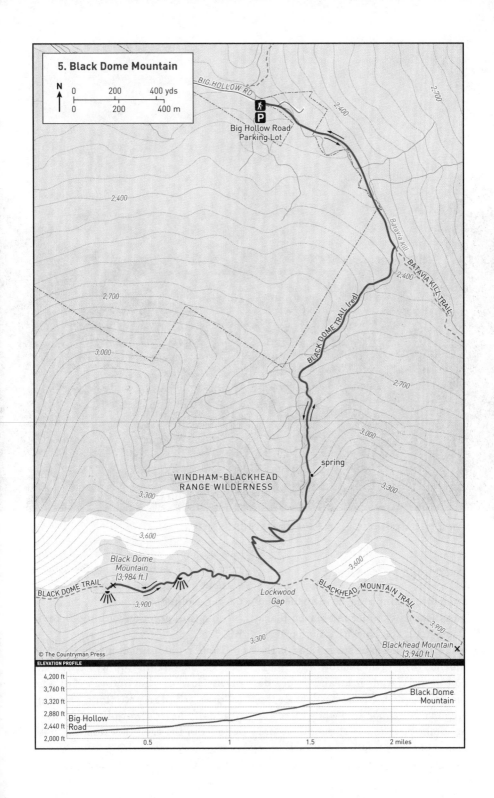

5. Black Dome Mountain

N

| 0 | 200 | 400 yds |
| 0 | 200 | 400 m |

BIG HOLLOW RD

Big Hollow Road
Parking Lot

2,400

2,700

2,400

Batavia Kill

BATAVIA KILL TRAIL

2,400

BLACK DOME TRAIL (red)

2,700

3,000

2,700

3,000

spring

WINDHAM-BLACKHEAD
RANGE WILDERNESS

3,300

3,300

3,600

Black Dome
Mountain
(3,984 ft.)

3,600

BLACK DOME TRAIL

Lockwood
Gap

BLACKHEAD MOUNTAIN TRAIL

3,900

3,300

3,900

Blackhead Mountain
(3,940 ft.)

© The Countryman Press

ELEVATION PROFILE

4,200 ft	
3,760 ft	
3,320 ft	Black Dome
	Mountain
2,880 ft	
Big Hollow	
2,440 ft	Road
2,000 ft	
	0.5 1 1.5 2 miles

VIEW OF THE BLACKHEAD RANGE FROM THE ABANDONED CORTINA MOUNTAIN SKI AREA

THE TRAIL

From the parking area, head up the road into the forest on the red-blazed Black Dome Trail. You'll pass through private land right away, so be sure to stay on the trail and respect the landowner's rights. Follow the trail as it meanders beside the Batavia Kill. The trail will cross the stream a few times, and while there are no footbridges to assist you, there are plenty of rocks that you can pick your way across on. In times of high runoff, it may be impossible to cross the stream without getting wet. Follow the trail for 0.6 mile, climbing gradually, until you reach a trail junction with the Batavia Kill Trail.

Turn right and continue on the Black Dome Trail. You will leave the main flow of the Batavia Kill and follow a tributary, climbing about as gradually as you were before. Half a mile from the trail junction, the path veers away from the tributary and begins to climb more steeply. The forest here is mostly composed of mixed hardwoods. If the leaves are off the trees, you may be able to see that you are beginning to enter a corridor between two shoulders of the range. Continue climbing for another mile, eventually switchbacking through an overgrown craggy section toward the top of the ridge.

When you reach Lockwood Gap—the saddle between Blackhead and Black Dome—turn right and continue going uphill, staying on the Black Dome Trail. For the next quarter of a mile, the trail is quite steep. You will come to a few small switchbacks, but for the most part the trail goes straight up, sometimes leading you up and over rocky berms through gaps in the ledges. You may be able to see Blackhead Mountain behind you through

the trees, depending on what time of year you are hiking. There is a decent view about halfway through this steep section, slightly off the trail to the left, looking south.

Eventually the trail will begin to level off as you crest the dome of the summit, entering the dense evergreen stands that give this mountain its name. In 0.6 mile from reaching the saddle, you will come to the summit, likely marked with a small cairn. There is yet another southward-facing view-point slightly past the summit off to the left, at the end of a short, well-defined herd path.

When you are finished on the summit, retrace your steps back to the saddle. Follow the red blazes from the saddle to the Batavia Kill and back to your vehicle at the parking area.

6

Blackhead Mountain

DISTANCE: 5 miles

TYPE: Loop

TOTAL ELEVATION GAIN: 1,790 feet

MAXIMUM ELEVATION: 3,940 feet

DIFFICULTY: Strenuous

HIKING TIME: 4 hours

The namesake for this grand northeastern range, Blackhead Mountain, at 3,940 feet sits well above the 3,500-foot Catskill high peak demarcation, and is tied with its westward brother Thomas Cole Mountain for fourth tallest summit in the Catskill Park. And while 40 feet shorter than Black Dome, Blackhead wins the prize for steepest climb out of the other two peaks in the range, climbing more than 1,000 feet in less than a mile. That being said, Blackhead offers spectacular views of the surrounding wilderness and is a real treat for hikers looking to push their limits. Because of the steep grade of the climb, hikers looking to tackle this peak in the winter months should check the weather and snowfall estimates, as well as come prepared with good traction devices. The trail near the summit can be very icy.

GETTING THERE

Take Exit 20 (Saugerties) from the New York State Thruway, then turn left onto NY-212/NY-32. At the traffic light, take a right onto NY-32 North. In 6 miles, continue straight onto NY-32A. In 1.9 miles, turn left onto Route 23A and drive up the winding mountain road toward Tannersville. After driving through Tannersville, turn right at the traffic light onto Hill Street (County Route 23C). Head north on NY-23C for 6.1 miles. Turn right onto County Route 40, and follow it until you come to the small town of Maplecrest, in about 2 miles. Veer right onto Big Hollow Road and drive for 4 miles. The parking area is at the very end of the road. Be aware that the last mile or so of this road is considered seasonal and is not maintained during winter months. During times of heavy snowfall, you may need

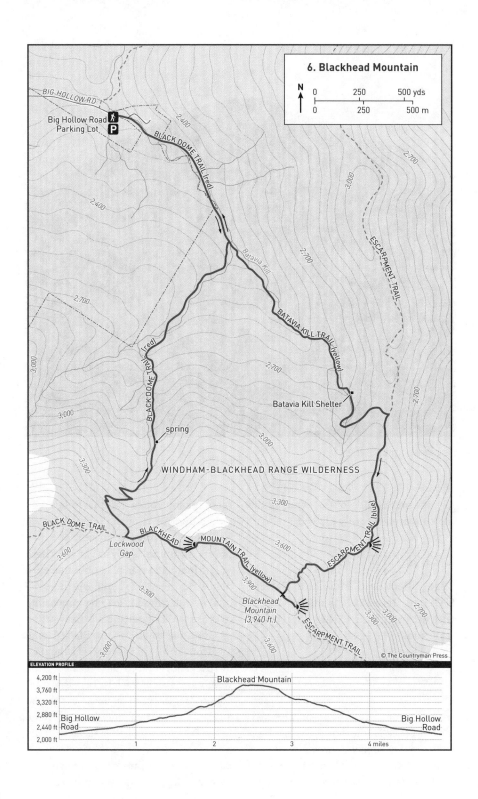

6. Blackhead Mountain

N

| 0 | 250 | 500 yds |
| 0 | 250 | 500 m |

BIG HOLLOW RD

Big Hollow Road
Parking Lot

2,400

BLACK DOME TRAIL (red)

2,700

3,000

Batavia Kill

2,700

BATAVIA KILL TRAIL (yellow)

ESCARPMENT TRAIL

2,700

2,700

2,400

BLACK DOME TRAIL (red)

2,700

Batavia Kill Shelter

spring

WINDHAM-BLACKHEAD RANGE WILDERNESS

3,000

3,000

3,300

3,000

3,300

3,300

ESCARPMENT TRAIL (blue)

BLACK DOME TRAIL

3,600

BLACKHEAD MOUNTAIN TRAIL (yellow)

3,600

Lockwood Gap

3,300

3,900

Blackhead Mountain (3,940 ft.)

ESCARPMENT TRAIL

3,000

2,700

3,300

3,000

3,600

© The Countryman Press

ELEVATION PROFILE

4,200 ft		Blackhead Mountain	
3,760 ft			
3,320 ft			
2,880 ft	Big Hollow		Big Hollow
2,440 ft	Road		Road
2,000 ft			

1   2   3   4 miles

LOOKING WEST TOWARD BLACK DOME

to park on the side of the road, as the parking area is rarely plowed.

GPS SHORTCUT

Type "Blackhead Mountain, Jewett, NY" into Google Maps and your GPS will navigate you to the appropriate trailhead.

THE TRAIL

The trailhead is at the end of the road, which enters the woods on the red-blazed Black Dome Trail. The trail follows the dirt road you drove in on for a short distance, briefly crossing private land before transitioning into an easily recognizable rocky trail that follows the twists and turns of the scenic Batavia Kill. You'll cross the stream at a few points, climbing gently as you do. There are no footbridges in place, but there are plenty of rocks to aid you. During periods of high runoff it may be impossible to cross without getting a little wet.

Continue to follow the Black Dome Trail for 0.6 miles until you reach the start of the yellow-blazed Batavia Kill Trail, which turns off to the left. Take this trail, continuing the gradual climb beside the stream. In about 0.6 mile, you will come to the Batavia Kill Shelter, located off the trail to the left in an area that is often wet. Stop and take a break if you wish, and then continue to follow the yellow blazes.

The trail will briefly level off a short distance past the shelter before turning sharply to the left. Be attentive to the trail markers, as it can be easy to miss this turn if you are absorbed in the beautiful scenery. After making the turn, the trail will begin to climb much more arduously than it has up until now. The trail will lead you uphill for about one-tenth of a mile before gaining the ridge and ending at the intersection of the Escarpment Trail.

At this point you have climbed roughly 700 feet in 1.5 miles. The summit is only 0.9 miles away, but you'll need to climb 1,090 feet to reach it! Turn right, following the blue blazes of the Escarpment Trail as it climbs uphill, getting steadily steeper as you continue. Use caution while you ascend, as the trail may be wet and rocky, or sometimes snowy and icy even in the spring and fall. Additionally, the drop-off can be very steep and sheer at certain points. Looking out to the left as you ascend will give you occasional spotty views of the Escarpment ridge as it progresses south.

The last tenth of a mile to the top is especially steep and will require you to use your hands to continue climbing. Take your time and use common sense. At the summit you will reach the junction of the yellow-blazed Blackhead Mountain Trail, which cuts to the right. Ignore this trail for now and continue down the Escarpment Trail for a few hundred feet without losing too much elevation and come to an excellent viewpoint, which faces east. On a clear day you may be able to see the Hudson River from here. When you are ready to resume hiking, return to the Blackhead Mountain Trail and follow it along the crest of the mountain. Begin descending along the same trail shortly. There is a nice vista on a sloping stone face, which you'll soon come to after beginning your descent, boasting superb views of neighboring Black Dome Mountain.

Continue descending to the col between Blackhead and Black Dome, meeting with the Black Dome Trail when you arrive. Turn right and follow the red blazes downhill as the trail switchbacks through a few steep sections before becoming less abrupt and begins following a tributary of the Batavia Kill. You will travel the Black Dome Trail for 1.4 miles before reaching the junction of the Batavia Kill Trail. At this point, turn left, continuing to follow the red blazes back to your vehicle, reminiscing as you walk beside the stream.

VIEW OF BLACKHEAD MOUNTAIN FROM BURNT KNOB

Colgate Lake to Dutcher Notch

DISTANCE: 8.6 miles

TYPE: Out and back

TOTAL ELEVATION GAIN: 385 feet

MAXIMUM ELEVATION: 2,550 feet

DIFFICULTY: Easy

HIKING TIME: 4 hours

Despite its length, the Colgate Lake to Dutcher Notch hike may be one of the easiest hikes you'll find in the eastern Catskills. Colgate Lake itself is a popular weekend destination in summer, crowded with families and swimmers. But a quarter-mile removed from the lake, the trail leading to Dutcher Notch is generally quiet—its lack of summits or vistas makes it far less popular than other nearby hikes. It is a lovely, peaceful hike nonetheless, a leisurely outing with diverse surroundings, winding through numerous meadows and bogs and over bridges. While it's not recommended to do this hike in the spring, due to wet conditions, the hike is ideal for the warmer summer days or to take in the fall foliage and can be cross-country skied in winter.

In addition to swimming and boating (Colgate Lake allows hand boats, but no motors), the lake is popular year-round for trout and features an accessible fishing platform. The lake is stocked annually.

GETTING THERE

Take Exit 20 (Saugerties) from the New York State Thruway, then turn left onto NY-212/NY-32. At the traffic light, take a right onto NY-32 North. In 6 miles, continue straight onto NY-32A. In 1.9 miles, turn left onto Route 23A and drive up the winding mountain road toward Tannersville. After driving through Tannersville, turn right at the traffic light onto Hill Street (County Route 23C). Head north about 3 miles to East Jewett. Make a right onto Route 78, then drive another 1.7 miles until you reach Colgate Lake. You will pass the larger of two DEC parking lots on the left side of the road just before the lake, but continue past down

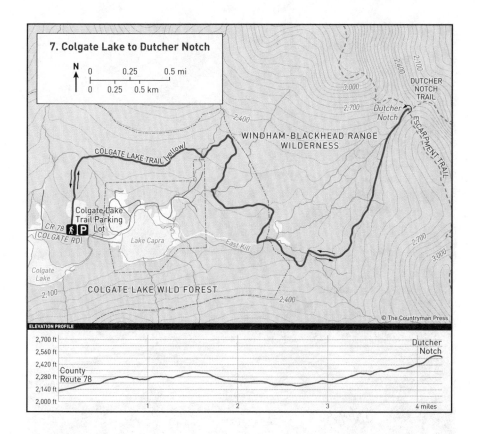

7. Colgate Lake to Dutcher Notch

ELEVATION PROFILE

the stone roadway to the second, smaller parking lot. This lot connects directly to the trailhead.

GPS SHORTCUT

Type "Colgate Lake" into Google Maps and your GPS will navigate you to the northern tip of the lake. Continue on Colgate Road for about half a mile to reach the parking lot on the left side of the road.

THE TRAIL

From the north end of the DEC parking lot, head out onto the trail into a large open field. Some of the best views of the hike come at the very beginning, with the surrounding mountains, including Blackhead and Arizona, dominating the horizon.

Walk for 0.2 mile through the field to reach the edge of the forest, where you will find the DEC registration box. The many oaks in this area cover the ground with acorns in early fall. As a result, there may be higher than average bear activity here during the autumn season, as bears will turn up to eat the acorns during the day.

From the registration box, the trail is flat and easy to follow. You will meander through a series of bogs and over bridges for the next several miles, reaching the first bridge around 1.2 miles into the hike. Ignore the logging roads, which lead onto private land,

INDUSTRIAL DEBRIS ALONG THE TRAIL TO DUTCHER NOTCH

and follow the yellow trail markers and signs.

Around 2.3 miles in, the trail cuts through the largest of the bogs, though it is not hard to traverse during drier months. From this clearing, you will be able to see West Stoppel Mountain in the background.

Upon leaving the bog, follow the arrow markers and take the trail to the left. You will soon come across the third bridge and a quiet, well-shaded stream. More bogs await after you leave this idyllic spot, until just after mile 3, where you will pass a large field. In this open, beautiful space, apple trees from an old orchard still grow. Off the trail in the field, there is a fire pit and small clearing for campers. Close to the trail, but hidden from sight, is a 15-foot waterfall. Listen closely for the sound of water, as the waterfall is very easy to miss.

The trail will begin to gain in elevation as it approaches Dutcher Notch, but it is never steep. To the left of the trail, the ground drops off sharply into a bank, with a large wall of rocks rising to the right.

Upon reaching Dutcher Notch, you will come to a prominent trail sign marking a four-way intersection of trails. The trail to the left heads north to Arizona Mountain and Blackhead Mountain. Right will take you to Stoppel Point and North Mountain.

When you are ready to return, retrace your steps back to your car.

INTERSECTION WITH THE ESCARPMENT TRAIL

Stoppel Point from Stork's Nest Road

DISTANCE: 8 miles	
TYPE: Out and back	
TOTAL ELEVATION GAIN: 2,290 feet	
MAXIMUM ELEVATION: 3,415 feet	
DIFFICULTY: Strenuous	
HIKING TIME: 4.5 hours	

With hiking destinations like Poet's Ledge, Inspiration Point, and Artist's Rock, the Catskills make it perfectly clear that this has been a place for contemplation and creativity over the years, but rarely are such philosophical tangents inspired by your GPS. Driving on the final leg to this remote Catskills trailhead, you'll spend a few miles on the coyly named "Hearts Content Road." One might assume the road's name implies contentedness: a street full of happy people in an idyllic mountain paradise. Yet the GPS chooses to pronounce it as "content"—as in the things the heart contains, a somewhat more philosophically ambiguous direction for the name of a small rural road. Perhaps, over the next several miles of climbing up the eastern escarpment of the Catskills, you'll have time to come to terms with the contents of your own heart, and whether you are indeed content with them.

One of the more obscure hikes in the northeastern Catskills, the simplest route to Stoppel Point starts from an isolated trailhead and makes a long, persistent ascent up to the top. From Stoppel Point, you will find a nice perch looking out over Blackhead, Black Dome, and Thomas Cole Mountains, and a second vista looking east toward the Hudson Valley. Adding to the highlights of the hike are the remains of an old plane crash, just off the trail near the summit. The solitude of the hike is appealing on its own, too, especially for the northeastern region of the park. The beginning of the hike is an easement on private land, and it crosses a private driveway just next to a home. It's thus perhaps for the best that the parking area on Stork's Nest Road does not hold more than a couple cars. In the off-season, or on a weekday, you might never see another hiker on the trail.

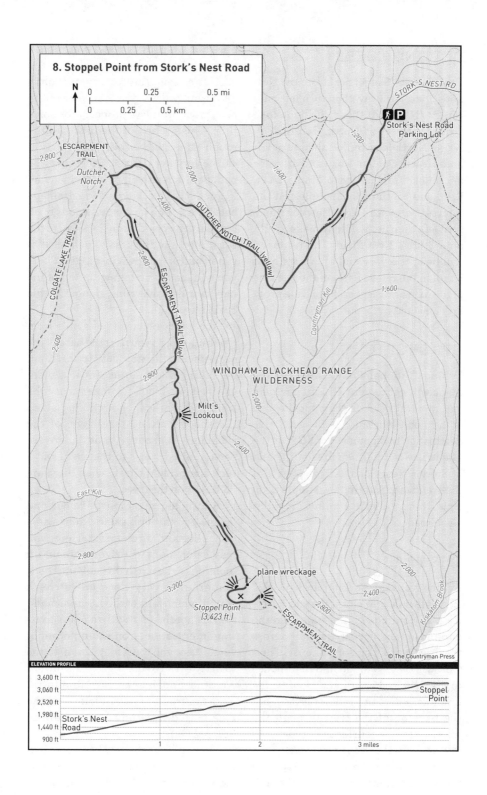

8. Stoppel Point from Stork's Nest Road

N

| 0 | 0.25 | 0.5 mi |
| 0 | 0.25 | 0.5 km |

STORK'S NEST RD

Stork's Nest Road
Parking Lot

ESCARPMENT
TRAIL

2,800

Dutcher
Notch

1,200

1,600

COLGATE LAKE TRAIL

2,000

DUTCHER NOTCH TRAIL (yellow)

Countryman Kill

1,600

2,400

2,800

ESCARPMENT TRAIL (blue)

2,400

2,800

WINDHAM-BLACKHEAD RANGE
WILDERNESS

2,000

Milt's
Lookout

2,400

East Kill

2,000

2,800

plane wreckage

2,000

Kiskatom Brook

3,200

×

Stoppel Point
(3,423 ft.)

2,800

2,400

ESCARPMENT TRAIL

© The Countryman Press

ELEVATION PROFILE

3,600 ft				
3,060 ft				Stoppel
2,520 ft				Point
1,980 ft				
1,440 ft	Stork's Nest			
900 ft	Road			
	1	2	3 miles	

GETTING THERE

Take Exit 20 (Saugerties) from the New York State Thruway, then turn left onto NY-212/NY-32. At the traffic light, take a right onto NY-32 North. Continue on NY-32 North for 11 miles, then turn left onto Hearts Content Road and drive for 3.8 miles. Turn left onto Maple Lawn Road and continue for 1.2 miles. At the intersection with Floyd Hawver Road, turn left, then immediately make a right onto Stork's Nest Road. The trailhead will be at the very end of Stork's Nest Road, in 0.6 miles. Park on the left side of the road and respect the private property adjacent to the lot.

GPS SHORTCUT

Typing "Stoppel Point" into Google Maps will cause your GPS to navigate you to a trailhead on the opposite side of the mountain. The closest searchable destination to input into your GPS is the Maple Lawn Hotel, which is at the end of Stork's Nest Road, 0.6 miles east of the trailhead. Alternately, simply drop a pin at the western terminus of Stork's Nest Road.

THE TRAIL

Across from the parking area, a DEC sign with mileages marks the start of the trail. To continue on the trail from the parking area, you must first walk across the driveway of someone's house. Their yard will be to your left and their house to the right, so head directly toward the tree line, where the yellow blazes mark the passage of the trail through the woods. Be very courteous of the owner and do not walk off the driveway.

Continue on the broad, easy trail for 0.2 mile, until you come to the trail register. Stop to register your hike, then continue over the wooden bridge across a stream. The trail begins slightly uphill, but gradually at first, and continues through private property for some time. This section of the hike is often rough after a heavy rain, and the trail can be very wet at times. Otherwise, the path here is relatively level and unchallenging, crisscrossing a wide drainage bed. This trough was once a woods road, but due to its position on the slope of the escarpment, it captures a great deal of runoff and is thus heavily eroded. Soon, you will mostly be hiking on top of the narrow ridge that runs alongside this drainage trough.

About three-quarters of a mile from the trailhead, as you near the base of the escarpment, the trail cuts to the right, beginning a steeper ascent to Dutcher's Notch. About 1.4 miles from the trailhead, you will begin hiking along the shady northeastern slope of the ridgeline. At about 1.5 miles, there are some limited views to the east from a rock alongside the trail when there are no leaves on the trees.

A little beyond, the trail levels and brings you through a dark, dense area of conifer and birch forest. Here, you may catch sight of Arizona Mountain looming to the north through the trees. You are now very close to Dutcher's Notch, which falls at the 1.8-mile mark. At the notch, you will reach a four-way intersection. Continuing straight would take you to Colgate Lake, to the west. The trail to the right heads toward Arizona and Blackhead Mountains. Take the trail to the left, following the blue-blazed Escarpment Trail toward Stoppel Point.

The trail immediately begins a moderate climb, but the steepest sections are yet to come. After this short uphill you will have an easy, relatively flat (and very pleasant) section of ridgeline to enjoy, before the steepest ascent begins at 2.6 miles. For a quarter mile, the trail climbs steeply, then very steeply. After the climb, however, you will be rewarded with a stroll through a very beautiful, mossy forest, and a short distance later, the best viewpoint of the hike.

Just under 3 miles from the trailhead, arrive at Milt's Lookout. Here, you will find a fantastic vista looking to the east. Take your time and enjoy a rest here, as the trail will soon tackle another steep uphill section before reaching the high point of the hike.

At 3.75 miles, as you are approaching the top of Stoppel Point, you will spot the wreckage of a plane crash through the trees. The wreckage is from 1983, when a pilot with a revoked student pilot's license flew too low over the mountain and went down in the woods.

Just past the site of the plane crash, you will arrive at a second, more limited vista, with views of Blackhead, Black Dome, and Thomas Cole Mountains. From here the trail makes a U-turn around the summit, and you will soon reach Stoppel Point, marked by another DEC trail sign. At Stoppel Point, another vista looks out east to the Hudson Valley.

When you are ready, retrace your steps to return to your car.

9

North Point

DISTANCE: 5.5 miles

TYPE: Lollipop

TOTAL ELEVATION GAIN: 900 feet

MAXIMUM ELEVATION: 3,100 feet

DIFFICULTY: Moderate

HIKING TIME: 3.5 hours

With stunning panoramic views covering 240 degrees of the horizon, North Point may boast one of the best vistas in all of the Catskills. From the large stone outcrop of the point, visitors will quickly see why this section of the mountains was once thick with hotels, and remains—even with the hotels and train lines long vanished—incredibly popular with tourists. Despite its location only a few miles north of the busy North-South Lake Campground, the trails leading to North Point are somewhat less crowded than others in the area, and the hike itself is not particularly challenging.

For those seeking to add on to their hike, Stoppel Point, to the north of North Point, can be reached with an additional 4 miles of hiking along the final stretch of trail, and various other shorter hikes can be explored around the North-South Lake area, including Artist's Rock and Newman's Ledge (#10) and Inspiration Point and Layman's Monument (#11). For all these reasons, North Point is a can't-miss Catskill hike.

GETTING THERE

Take Exit 20 (Saugerties) from the New York State Thruway, then turn left onto NY-212/NY-32. At the traffic light, take a right onto NY-32 North. In 6 miles, continue straight onto NY-32A. At Palenville, take a slight left onto NY-23A. The road climbs steeply up the mountain to Haines Falls. At Haines Falls, just after the post office, turn right onto North Lake Road. Continue for 3 miles. Just before the entrance to the North-South Lake Campground, turn right onto Scutt Road. Just down the road is a parking area, on the right. Watch for hikers crossing the road to the trailhead. The parking area is large, with two separate tiers,

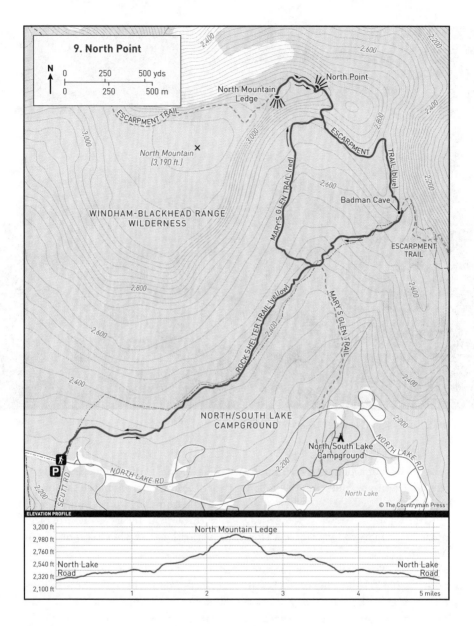

9. North Point

N
0   250   500 yds
0   250   500 m

North Point

North Mountain Ledge

ESCARPMENT TRAIL

North Mountain
(3,190 ft.)

ESCARPMENT TRAIL (blue)

MARY'S GLEN TRAIL (red)

Badman Cave

WINDHAM-BLACKHEAD RANGE WILDERNESS

ESCARPMENT TRAIL

ROCK SHELTER TRAIL (yellow)

MARY'S GLEN TRAIL

NORTH/SOUTH LAKE CAMPGROUND

North/South Lake Campground

NORTH LAKE RD.

SCUTT RD.

NORTH LAKE RD.

North Lake

© The Countryman Press

ELEVATION PROFILE

		North Mountain Ledge			
3,200 ft					
2,980 ft					
2,760 ft					
2,540 ft North Lake					North Lake
2,320 ft Road					Road
2,100 ft	1	2	3	4	5 miles

but it still fills up quickly due to the popularity of the hikes in this area.

GPS SHORTCUT

Direct your GPS to navigate to "North/South Lake Campground," and turn right onto Scutt Road immediately before the campground entrance.

THE TRAIL

From the parking area, turn left and walk up Scutt Road back to North Lake Road. There, turn left, away from the campground. A very short distance beyond, a trail sign indicates the start of the hike. This section of the trail is mostly level, and at the start crosses a

SUNRISE OVER THE HUDSON VALLEY FROM NORTH POINT

series of wooden planks over marshy ground. Continue, following the yellow blazes.

After 1.3 miles, arrive at a four-way intersection marked by a wooden sign. Turn left, onto the red-blazed Mary's Glen Trail. The trail begins to climb more steeply here, but the grade is still fairly moderate. Be careful of your footing as you ascend, as rocks in this area can remain wet even when it has not recently rained.

Soon the grade will level again, and you will hike parallel to a small stream to the right of the trail. About half a mile from the trail intersection, the trail enters a conifer forest. Continue until you reach the intersection with the blue-blazed Escarpment Trail. Go left.

Here, the trail climbs abruptly to North Point, approximately a quarter of a mile from the intersection. Ascending through a forest of white birch trees, with a few short scrambles up rock ledges, you will come to the first viewpoint on a ledge slightly southeast of North Point. The views here may be slightly overgrown during the summer, but this vista is only a preview of the far more dramatic and open views that you will find above.

Pull yourself up the final short scramble, and you will find yourself at North Point—a massive stone plateau with outcroppings mostly unobstructed by foliage, providing a variety of views to the southeast, east toward the Hudson, and even to the north. Enjoy this unique perspective over North-South Lake and the site of the former Catskill Mountain House.

Only a quarter mile past North Point is North Mountain Ledge, which offers a similar vantage to North Point, and thus more stunning views. Between these small areas of ledges, it can seem as if the whole of the Catskills is spread out before you.

When you are ready to head back, return down to the intersection just below North Point. Continue straight, staying on the blue trail. About 0.6 mile from North Point, you will come to another large stone plateau, though the views here are limited due to tree cover. The trail continues to the left.

Shortly after, you will reach a large rock formation known as Badman Cave. (Fortunately, at the time of this writing, there was no man living in the cave, bad or otherwise.) Just beyond the cave is another intersection. Take the yellow-blazed trail heading to the right. In another half mile, you will intersect which the red-blazed Mary's Glen Trail that you originally took toward North Point.

Stay straight, following the trail as the red and yellow blazes briefly overlap. A short distance beyond, the trail splits once again, as you complete the head of the loop. Follow the yellow blazes to the left to retrace the first leg of the hike and return to North Lake Road and the parking area.

VIEW OF NORTH LAKE FROM NORTH POINT

Artist's Rock and Newman's Ledge

DISTANCE: 2.1 miles	
TYPE: Out and back	
TOTAL ELEVATION GAIN: 310 feet	
MAXIMUM ELEVATION: 2,460 feet	
DIFFICULTY: Easy	
HIKING TIME: 1.5 hours	

With easy access, wide well-marked trails, and an abundance of incredible vistas, it's no surprise that the North-South Lake area historically has been and still remains a popular destination for tourists and hikers alike. While the area is small enough that you can see most of it in a day, there are numerous trails and landmarks that warrant further exploration, so set aside plenty of time to enjoy the natural beauty here. There may be no better views out over the Hudson Valley than from the vistas along this hike.

The route described below will lead you to aptly named Artist's Rock and scenic Newman's Ledge, passing a few other viewpoints along the way. This easy hike can be combined with visits to other landmarks as time allows, given the numerous trails that wind all throughout the North-South Lake area.

GETTING THERE

Take Exit 20 (Saugerties) from the New York State Thruway, then turn left onto NY-212/NY-32. At the traffic light, take a right onto NY-32 North. In 6 miles, continue straight onto NY-32A. At Palenville, take a slight left onto NY-23A. The road climbs steeply up the mountain to Haines Falls. At Haines Falls, just after the post office, turn right onto North Lake Road. Continue for 3 miles. You will reach the campground entrance. Here, you will have to pay the fee for day access to the campground. Once past the entrance, continue on North Lake Road to the final, large parking area, east of the lake.

GPS SHORTCUT

Direct your GPS to navigate you to "North/South Lake Campground." Once past the entrance, continue on

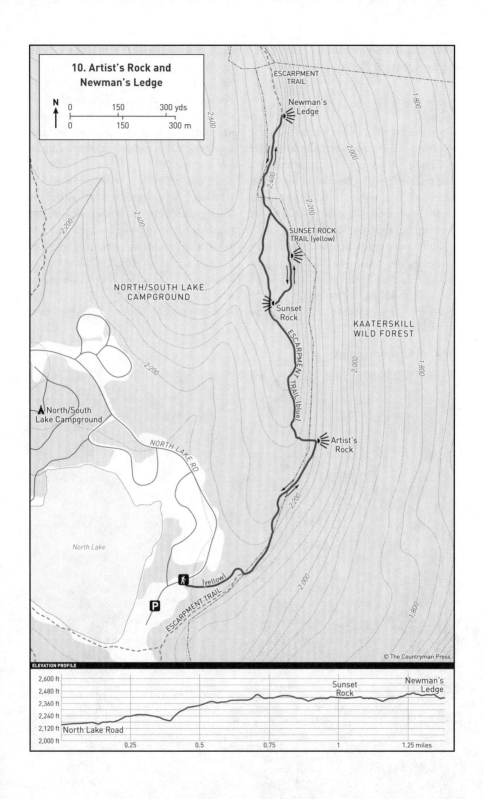

10. Artist's Rock and Newman's Ledge

N
| 0 | 150 | 300 yds |
| 0 | 150 | 300 m |

ESCARPMENT
TRAIL

Newman's
Ledge

2,600

1,800

2,000

2,400

2,200

SUNSET ROCK
TRAIL (yellow)

NORTH/SOUTH LAKE
CAMPGROUND

KAATERSKILL
WILD FOREST

Sunset
Rock

2,200

ESCARPMENT TRAIL (blue)

2,000

1,800

North/South
Lake Campground

NORTH LAKE RD

Artist's
Rock

2,200

North Lake

(yellow)

ESCARPMENT TRAIL

2,000

1,800

© The Countryman Press

ELEVATION PROFILE

			Sunset Rock	Newman's Ledge

2,600 ft
2,480 ft
2,360 ft
2,240 ft
2,120 ft — North Lake Road
2,000 ft

0.25   0.5   0.75   1   1.25 miles

North Lake Road to the final, large parking area, east of the lake.

THE TRAIL

From the large parking lot, walk to the road you drove in on and follow it to the trailhead, just above the parking area. The trail enters the woods on the right-hand side of the road. It is easy to spot: There is a wooden barrier blocking off the trail to vehicular traffic.

Follow the yellow blazes. After a short distance, you will cut to the right to join the blue-blazed Escarpment Trail. Here you will find the trail register.

At about a quarter mile into the hike, you will reach a modestly challenging rock scramble, but it is short and easily navigated even by inexperienced day-trippers. The trail afterward will continue to work its way over, around, and through unique rock formations, which present their own pleasant scenery.

In 0.4 miles, you will arrive at Artist's Rock, with views out to the Hudson Valley and beyond. Soak in the views (and if you don't yet feel inspired to take up oil painting, perhaps you could visit Inspiration Point, Guide #11, in tandem with this). When you are ready, continue north.

The trail at times climbs moder-

EARLY AUTUMN IN THE CATSKILLS

KAATERSKILL HIGH PEAK AND ROUND TOP MOUNTAIN

ately uphill, but it is not strenuous. At 0.85 mile you will reach an intersection with a yellow side trail. This trail runs parallel to the blue-blazed path that you have been on and doubles back along the ridgeline to the south, leading to Sunset Rock and various overlooks with views similar to Artist's Rock. You can take this side trail now or on your return from Newman's Ledge. It adds only a short distance to your hike but offers stunning views over North Lake.

For now, continue straight at the intersection, following the blue blazes north, toward Newman's Ledge. Immediately after the intersection, the trail spikes uphill for a short distance before leveling out. Soon you will come to Newman's Ledge, which offers similar views to Artist's Rock, but with more dramatic rock protrusions out over the cliff face and better views to the north.

When you are ready to return, retrace your steps to the parking area.

Inspiration Point and Layman's Monument

DISTANCE: 4.7 miles

TYPE: Lollipop

TOTAL ELEVATION GAIN: 190 feet

MAXIMUM ELEVATION: 2,430 feet

DIFFICULTY: Easy

HIKING TIME: 3.5 hours

While North-South Lake—historic home to several famous Catskill hotels, and now grounds for a large camping area—is one of the most popular Catskill destinations on its own, the trails that surround the lake offer an equal draw. Together, this area holds some of the richest scenery in the park, and these views happen to be some of the most accessible, too. On the Escarpment Trail that skirts the lake, vistas hit one after another, the sites and history lessons like a "Best Of" for the region. On this loop hike exploring the trails southwest of North-South Lake, you will experience some of the most dramatic of the vistas overlooking Kaaterskill Clove at Inspiration Point and Sunset Rock. At Layman's Monument, a break in the trees gives an unusual perspective over the clove: straight on, as if floating above the notch between mountains. Here, the Frank D. Layman Memorial commemorates the firefighter who died at this site on August 10, 1900, fighting to protect the area from a blaze.

GETTING THERE

Take Exit 20 (Saugerties) from the New York State Thruway, then turn left onto NY-212/NY-32. At the traffic light, take a right onto NY-32 North. In 6 miles, continue straight onto NY-32A. At Palenville, take a slight left onto NY-23A. The road climbs steeply up the mountain to Haines Falls. At Haines Falls, just after the post office, turn right onto North Lake Road. Continue for 3 miles. Just before the entrance to the North-South Lake Campground, turn right onto Scutt Road. Just down the road is a parking area on the right. Watch for hikers crossing the road to the trailhead. The parking area is large, with two separate tiers,

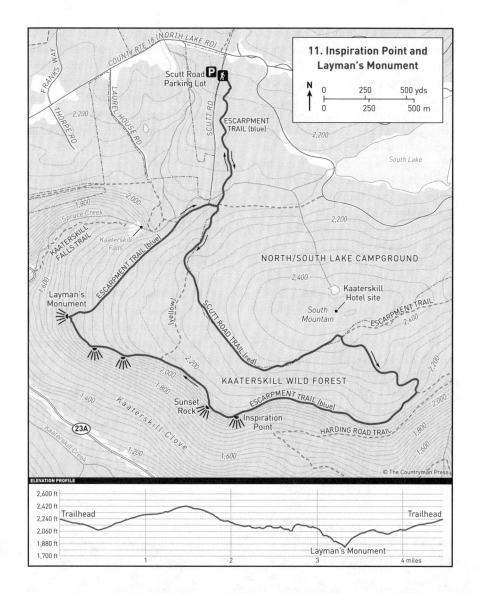

11. Inspiration Point and Layman's Monument

N

| 0 | 250 | 500 yds |
| 0 | 250 | 500 m |

FRANKS WAY

COUNTY RTE 18 (NORTH LAKE RD)

Scutt Road Parking Lot

THORPE RD

LAUREL HOUSE RD

SCUTT RD

ESCARPMENT TRAIL (blue)

2,200

2,200

South Lake

2,200

1,800

2,000

Spruce Creek

KAATERSKILL FALLS TRAIL

Kaaterskill Falls

ESCARPMENT TRAIL (blue)

2,200

NORTH/SOUTH LAKE CAMPGROUND

2,400

Kaaterskill Hotel site

1,600

Layman's Monument

South Mountain

ESCARPMENT TRAIL

2,400

(yellow)

SCUTT ROAD TRAIL (red)

2,000

2,200

KAATERSKILL WILD FOREST

1,400

1,800

Kaaterskill Clove

Sunset Rock

ESCARPMENT TRAIL (blue)

2,000

23A

Inspiration Point

HARDING ROAD TRAIL

1,800

1,600

Kaaterskill Creek

1,200

1,600

© The Countryman Press

ELEVATION PROFILE

| 2,600 ft |
| 2,420 ft |
| 2,240 ft | Trailhead |
| 2,060 ft |
| 1,880 ft |
| 1,700 ft |

Trailhead

Layman's Monument

1   2   3   4 miles

but it still fills up quickly due to the popularity of the hikes in this area.

GPS SHORTCUT

Direct your GPS to navigate to "North/South Lake Campground," and turn right onto Scutt Road immediately before the campground entrance.

THE TRAIL

From the parking area on Scutt Road, cross the street that you drove in on to find the trailhead, marked by blue blazes. Follow the Scutt Trail heading south. The path starts off level, though somewhat rocky and crisscrossed by roots.

At 0.4 mile, you will cross an old railroad grade running east–west. The tracks here once brought passengers directly from the valley below up into the Catskill Park region. Just after the railroad grade, you will come to the trail register.

Shortly after the trail register, at 0.5 mile, you will reach a four-way intersection. This is the first of many intersections you will encounter on this hike: The North-South Lake area is thick with trails and opportunities to forge new loops, but most trails are very well marked, with wooden signs indicating landmarks and distances at prominent intersections. To your right is the trail you will return on at the end of your loop. For now, stay straight, following the red blazes. The trail will now begin to ascend slightly uphill.

In a quarter mile, you will come to another intersection with a yellow-blazed trail. Keep to the left, following the red blazes. After another 0.75 mile of easy hiking, you will come to a multisection intersection that is the most disorienting portion of this hike. An unmarked trail to your left leads toward the site of the former Kaaterskill Hotel. Little remains of the old structures, but this unmarked narrow pathway does offer a nice short loop through the woods and the scant sights of the former mountain getaway. From this same intersection, only a few steps beyond the first unmarked trail, the aqua-green-blazed Long Path diverges in two directions. To the left, the blue-blazed trail will take you toward North Lake and eastern sections of the ridgeline, where spots like Boulder Rock offer views out to the Hudson Valley.

Take the trail to the right, heading south on the blue blazes. After half a mile, turn right again onto a flat pathway, still following the blue blazes. Shortly after this, turn left to stay on the trail—the path heading straight from this intersection is a horse path cutting back toward the beginning of your hike.

Very soon, views will begin to open up

LOOKING ACROSS KAATERSKILL CLOVE

LAYMAN'S MONUMENT OFFERS A VIEW UP KAATERSKILL CLOVE

to the left of the trail, offering glimpses of Kaaterskill Clove. There are many scenic viewpoints and dramatic ledges here that make for a perfect lunch site. At Inspiration Point and Sunset Rock, there are a number of ledges where you can sit, catch your breath, and take photographs of the dramatic scenery surrounding you.

Stay straight at the intersection with the yellow trail, and continue on, past several more ledges and overlooks, to Layman's Monument. Here, the foliage opens up, allowing a glimpse of the hikers making their way down NY-23A to Kaaterskill Falls, and the clove stretching westward toward Haines Falls.

At Layman's Monument, the trail hooks to the right. Follow the blue blazes. After another half mile of hiking, you will begin to see signs for the side trail leading to the viewing station above Kaaterskill Falls. This is a short side trail that can be added on to your hike for an opportunity to see the famous waterfall from another angle.

After the waterfall side path, be mindful of the private property that borders the trail on the north side. Continue on toward the intersection with the trail register. Here you will reach the final leg of the hike, leading back to the parking area. Follow the blue trail you hiked in on north to return to your car.

Kaaterskill Falls

DISTANCE: 1 mile

TYPE: Out and back

DIFFICULTY: Easy

HIKING TIME: < 1 hour

Kaaterskill Falls, one of the tallest waterfalls in New York State, is accessible by a short hiking trail off a main road, and thus easily earns the distinction of being one of the most visited and best-known tourist destinations in the Catskills. The two stages of Kaaterskill Falls total 260 feet in height. Immensely popular with travelers over the last century, the falls are also one of America's oldest well-known tourist attractions, brought to notoriety by various books, poems, and paintings in the early nineteenth century.

Many paths and wooden viewing stations that once allowed tourists access to all parts of the falls have since been removed or destroyed, and today it is extremely dangerous to try to reach parts of the waterfall away from the designated hiking trail. Indeed, there are injuries and even deaths almost every year as a result of hikers going off-trail, ignoring warning signs, exploring the most dangerous sections of the waterfall, and losing their footing and falling.

The Catskills can claim the odd distinction of being one of the few tourist destinations in America that is less developed and perhaps even less popular in the modern age than a century ago. Nonetheless, the ghost of tourism past still lingers heavily in this area, and other nearby hikes like Artist's Rock and Newman's Ledge (Guide #10) and Inspiration Point and Layman's Monument (Guide #11) provide a glimpse at the once-bustling hotel business that dominated life around Kaaterskill Falls and North-South Lake.

GETTING THERE

Take Exit 20 (Saugerties) from the New York State Thruway, then turn left onto

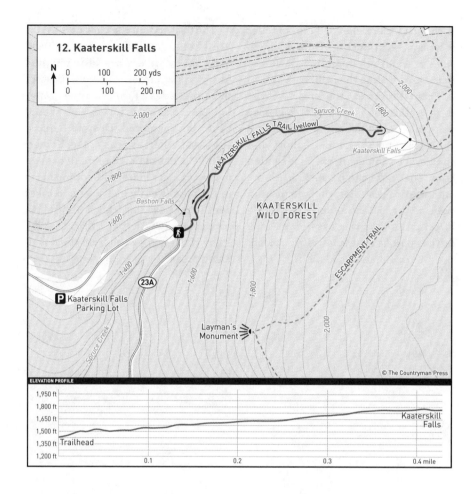

12. Kaaterskill Falls

N
0   100   200 yds
0   100   200 m

Spruce Creek
2,000
1,800
KAATERSKILL FALLS TRAIL (yellow)
Kaaterskill Falls
1,800
Bastion Falls
1,600
KAATERSKILL
WILD FOREST
ESCARPMENT TRAIL
1,400
23A
1,600
1,800
P Kaaterskill Falls
Parking Lot
Spruce Creek
Layman's
Monument
2,000

© The Countryman Press

ELEVATION PROFILE

1,950 ft
1,800 ft
1,650 ft
1,500 ft   Kaaterskill
1,350 ft Trailhead   Falls
1,200 ft
        0.1   0.2   0.3   0.4 mile

NY-212/NY-32. At the traffic light, take a right onto NY-32 North. In 6 miles, continue straight onto NY-32A. Follow NY-32A for 2 miles. In the small town of Palenville, make a slight left onto NY-23A and follow the road as it enters the Catskill Park. From here, the road climbs steeply up the mountain. You will notice the trailhead for the falls on the right side of the road at a sharp bend, but the main parking area is further still up the road. Continue for a few hundred feet to find the parking area on the left side of the road.

GPS SHORTCUT

Type "Kaaterskill Falls Parking" into Google Maps and your GPS will navigate you to the appropriate parking area.

THE TRAIL

From the parking area, walk down the left side of the road for 0.25 mile, keeping to the mountainside and off the road as much as possible. There is no dedicated pedestrian walkway, and at points you will have to quickly walk along the road itself. Walk downhill to the access point for the trail, at the bend in the road. Here, the road crosses over a stream, with Bastion Falls—a much smaller waterfall—tumbling down the rocky area next to the trailhead.

From the road, the trail weaves through the woods for a relatively easy half mile before reaching Kaaterskill Falls. Though the trail is short and simple, you should still exercise caution here: The rocks can be slick. With the number of tourists here making the trail seem closer to Central Park than a wild forest excursion, it is easy to get hurt on the approach to the falls if you forget that this is still untamed nature.

The trail ends at the base of the falls. While stunning views can be found here, many hikers are still tempted to try to get closer, or to climb up to the large ledge of this two-tier waterfall. Such a climb is unsafe and should never be attempted. Despite being a short and otherwise easy hike, Kaaterskill Falls has claimed more lives than many other, far more challenging hikes in the area. Nearly every year, a hiker venturing past the trail is injured in some way. It is not worth the risk—enjoy Kaaterskill Falls from the designated areas.

Poet's Ledge

DISTANCE: 7 miles

TYPE: Out and back

TOTAL ELEVATION GAIN: 1,650 feet

MAXIMUM ELEVATION: 2,350 feet

DIFFICULTY: Difficult

HIKING TIME: 4 hours

The view from Poet's Ledge is one of the best in the region, but the hike to the vista is a little more complicated. You'll have to work more than usual to reach the viewing area, following an arduous ascent up an old dirt road, sandwiched between a short roadwalk at the beginning and a segment of relatively easy walking near the top. Don't let the climb discourage you, though! This is an excellent hike offering a good deal of solitude in addition to the wonderful view from the ledge. At times the trail crosses private land. As always, be courteous and respect the landowner's rights by staying on the designated trail.

There are blueberry bushes very close to the viewpoint, and when the fruit is ripe the area is frequently visited by black bears that can be quite protective of this plentiful food source. Be alert, exercise caution, and make sure you are educated on what to do in the event of a bear encounter.

GETTING THERE

Take Exit 20 (Saugerties) from the New York State Thruway, then turn left onto NY-212/NY-32. At the traffic light, take a right onto NY-32 North. In 6 miles, continue straight onto NY-32A. Follow NY-32A for 2 miles. In the small town of Palenville, make a slight left onto NY-23A and follow the road as it enters the Catskill Park. The parking area will be on your right just after crossing the park boundary, in about 100 feet. It is a small gravel lot, nestled in the trees a short distance off the road. If you reach a bridge crossing Kaaterskill Creek, you have gone too far. Do not park at the turnoff near the bridge.

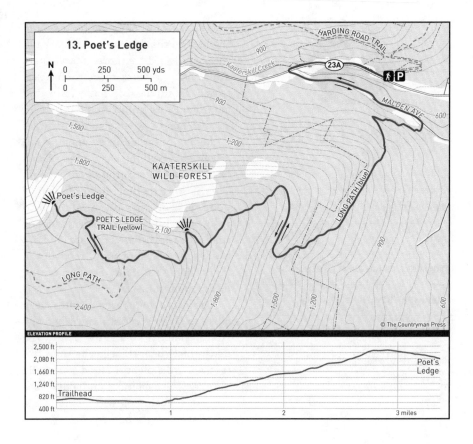

GPS SHORTCUT

Search Google Maps for "NY-23A & White Road." The parking lot is 0.2 mile up NY-23A to the west.

THE TRAIL

From the parking area, head to the road and turn right, following the street further into the park. The road can be busy at times, so stay on the shoulder and be cautious. You will walk alongside the road for 0.3 mile, crossing the bridge over Kaaterskill Creek when you come to it. On the other side of the bridge, turn left and cross the road. Once you cross the road, you will turn sharply to the left and follow a short segment of pavement heading back in the direction you came, this

time on the opposite side of the creek. At the end of this short paved area, enter the woods, passing a guardrail, and continue to follow the remnants of an abandoned road for half a mile as it skirts the bank of Kaaterskill Creek.

When you emerge from the woods, walk a short distance onto Malden Avenue and turn right, heading uphill on a gravel road grade. There are aquagreen Long Path blazes marking the way. Shortly after turning onto the gravel road, you will turn right again at a DEC trail sign and head back into the woods, eventually passing a metal gate. This is the start of the long, steady climb out of Kaaterskill Clove. You will stay on this grassy dirt road for 0.6 mile, ascending the entire time. This section of the trail is on private land, so stay on

THE VIEW FROM POET'S LEDGE LOOKING WEST

the trail. Follow the aqua-green Long Path blazes, and veer to the right, leaving the road grade and continuing your climb on a footpath. When you cross the Kaaterskill Wild Forest boundary, blue trail markers will join the green Long Path blazes. The trail makes a hard turn to the right 0.3 mile after leaving the road grade, and then levels out for another 0.3 mile.

Begin another steady ascent as the trail bends to the left, about half a mile after leaving the grassy road. Your course will take you up and over several very large stone ledges that cross the trail, like an oversized staircase. The trail will continue to steadily gain elevation, weaving through the forest. Roughly half a mile after resuming your ascent, you will come to a small open clearing on the right side of the trail. From here you can catch views of the cliffs on the opposite side of Kaaterskill Clove and see down into the valley below.

Continue to follow the trail uphill. The grade will begin to level shortly after you leave the ledge, and in about 0.3 mile you will come to a trail branching off to the right, marked by a sign. This is the spur trail that leads to Poet's Ledge. You are now at the high point of this hike, 2.1 miles from leaving Malden Avenue. Turn right onto the trail and begin following the yellow blazes. The trail begins a moderate descent, winding through serene forest and passing a couple exposed rock ledges on the way.

After dropping 200 vertical feet over the course of half a mile, you will arrive at Poet's Ledge. The yellow-blazed trail comes to an end here. This vista faces northwest, offering panoramic views of the mountainous landscape spreading out before you. The ledge drops off significantly, so be careful as you explore and enjoy the view. Make sure to bring a notebook and pen with you on the hike, as it is required that you write a poem from this vantage. (Of course, to complete the creative trifecta, you will also have to hike nearby Artist's Rock, Guide #10, and Inspiration Point, Guide #11.)

When you are ready to leave, walk back up the yellow-blazed trail and turn left onto the Long Path. Retrace your footsteps back to the parking area. Be careful as you descend to the road grade, as rocky portions of the trail can be slippery, especially when wet.

Kaaterskill High Peak from Gillespie Road

DISTANCE: 6.4 miles

TYPE: Out and back

TOTAL ELEVATION GAIN: 1,305 feet

MAXIMUM ELEVATION: 3,655 feet

DIFFICULTY: Easy

HIKING TIME: 3.5 hours

The easternmost Catskill mountain over 3,500 feet in elevation, Kaaterskill High Peak—with its distinct, easily recognizable profile and storied past—is an excellent hike for explorers and historians alike. The popular nineteenth-century painter Thomas Cole captured the mountain's figure in several paintings, and this influence would help to establish Kaaterskill High Peak and neighboring Round Top Mountain as enduring icons of the Catskill Mountains. The peak was once thought to be the highest point in the Catskills, until resurveying determined it to be the twenty-third tallest peak, more than 500 feet shorter than the actual high point on Slide Mountain.

The hike described below is an easy approach from the south that entails a fairly painless climb along the lightly used snowmobile trail that circles the peak. The last half mile to the top is on an unmaintained section of trail that is fairly steep. Along the way you will experience firsthand some of the economic history of the mountain, and on the summit you will see the remaining wreckage of a plane crash that occurred in the late twentieth century. There are a few views at various points from which you can survey the surrounding landscape, looking north and south.

GETTING THERE

Take Exit 20 (Saugerties) from the New York State Thruway, then turn left onto NY-212/NY-32. At the traffic light, take a right onto NY-32 North. In 6 miles, continue straight onto NY-32A. In 1.9 miles, turn left onto Route 23A, and drive up the winding mountain road toward Tannersville. Remain on NY-23A for 6 miles before turning left onto Clum Hill Road,

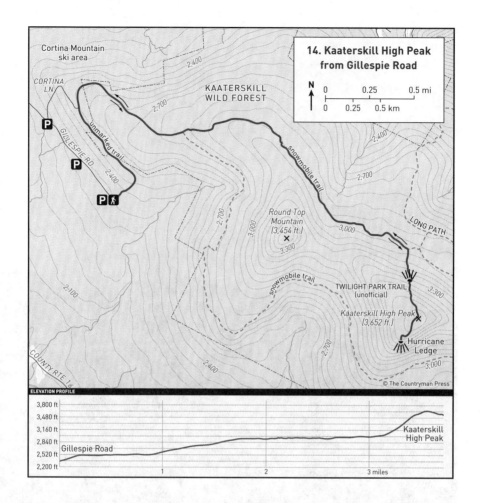

about a mile before reaching downtown Tannersville. Follow Clum Hill Road to a T intersection and turn left, taking Gillespie Road for about a mile until it ends at a grassy parking area on the edge of a field. The last half mile is a rocky dirt road that can be difficult to navigate if your vehicle sits low to the ground. There is additional parking roughly halfway up the dirt road, and just before Cortina Lane. Do not turn onto Cortina Lane, as this is a private driveway. You will have to walk to the end of Gillespie Road if you park at either of these two areas.

GPS SHORTCUT

Search Google Maps for "Gillespie Road, Elka Park, NY." Your GPS will take you halfway up Gillespie Road. Continue to the parking area where the road ends.

THE TRAIL

From the parking lot at the end of Gillespie Road, pick up an old rutted dirt road next to a wooden fence and follow it, heading into the woods along the edge of an overgrown field. Although the trail

THE EASTERN HALF OF THE DEVIL'S PATH, FROM HURRICANE LEDGE

here is unmarked, it is generally fairly easy to follow. You will keep on this path as it heads uphill for a short distance, about 0.2 mile. At this point the woods road will turn to the left and level off. You will walk parallel to the eastern shoulder of Round Top Mountain, which rises to your right, through forest predominantly composed of maple and beech trees. There is a fair amount of blowdown on this unmarked road, and you will occasionally have to leave the

traversing these soupy areas along the edge of the road.

About 0.9 mile from the parking area, you will emerge from the woods into a clearing where two gravel roads meet. These are the ruins of Cortina Mountain ski area, which was in business from 1975 to the early 2000s. There are a few dilapidated buildings still standing, as well as a ski lift system. From here you can see the Hunter Mountain ski area off to the west, as well as the East Jewett Range of mountains to the northwest. A small stand of trees blocks the view of Hunter village, which sits directly between these two mountain ranges. There is also a good view that faces north, looking out from the fern-covered ski lift swath, where you can see the Blackhead Range.

Reenter the woods by walking under the ski lift cables on a continuation of the dirt road, passing a run-down building on your left. You will pass through a gate immediately upon stepping back into the woods. This marks the start of a snowmobile trail that runs out and around the summits of Kaaterskill High Peak and Round Top Mountain. You will start to see markers along the side of the trail. Some of them will be red, and some of them will be yellow, but they both mark the same trail. Continue to follow the snowmobile trail for about 0.75 mile, climbing gradually on rocky road grade until you reach a sign that announces the start of the loop portion of the trail. Veer left and continue hiking along the snowmobile trail, which maintains the same relatively flat grade as before.

main grade of the trail to skirt around some of the bigger fallen trees, but you will always return to the uneven road to continue. Certain sections of this path can be muddy depending on the time of year, but you should have no problem

After 1.6 miles, you will come to a trail that bends to the right, marked by a small cairn. This is the unmaintained path that leads to the summit. If you reach a blue-blazed trail coming in on your left, you have gone too far and will have to backtrack about a tenth of a mile. Turn onto the unmaintained trail and begin climbing much more aggressively. The trail is rocky and steep, sending you past large overgrown boulders and through gaps in the ledges to ascend. You may need to use your hands in certain areas. There are a few weatherworn blue blazes still hung on the trees, and occasionally small cairns to mark the path, but it is easy to distinguish nonetheless. After about 0.3 mile of intense climbing, the grade will begin to lessen, and you should be able to cover ground much more quickly. The forest will transition to mostly balsam, spruce, and birch, and the trail will narrow. There is a decent view through

a small break in the trees about 0.2 mile from the summit, through which you can catch a glimpse of the Blackhead Range to the north.

Half a mile after turning onto the unmaintained trail, you will reach the summit, a wide grassy clearing with a herd path heading straight on and another breaking off to the right. There are no views from here, but there is a piece of wreckage from a plane crash that occurred on the mountain in the 1980s, as well as a few USGS markers that you can find if you look around.

Pick up the herd path that goes straight on and follow it for about a tenth of a mile, heading south as it descends nearly 200 feet. It may be hard to follow, so take your time and

DISTANT KAATERSKILL HIGH PEAK

AIRPLANE WRECKAGE ON THE SUMMIT OF KAATERSKILL HIGH PEAK

reassess your route often. At the end of this little trail is Hurricane Ledge, a small rock outcropping that boasts 180-degree views of the surrounding landscape. To your left you can see Kaaterskill Clove, and to your right you can see Platte Clove, Indian Head Mountain, and Twin Mountain, the start of the Devil's Path range. On a clear day you should be able to make out the fire tower on Overlook Mountain, which sits behind Indian Head, slightly to the left. The Hudson River serves as a nice backdrop to the scenery, stretching from north to south through the distant countryside below. This is an excellent place to enjoy a snack and take a break before making the trek back to the trailhead.

To return to your car, reverse your course and take the unmaintained trail downhill to the snowmobile path. Turn left and follow the red and yellow markers to the old ski area, at which point you will join the run-down forest road and walk its length back to the parking lot.

II.

EASTERN CENTRAL

15

Huckleberry Point

DISTANCE: 4.8 miles

TYPE: Out and back

TOTAL ELEVATION GAIN: 645 feet

MAXIMUM ELEVATION: 2,545 feet

DIFFICULTY: Easy

HIKING TIME: 3 hours

The eastern edges of the Catskills are rich with overlooks—indeed, some of the best views in all the park. Here, dramatic cloves and escarpments offer vantages that often top the impact of some mountain summit vistas, with steeper drop-offs and bird's-eye views into the valleys below. The hike to Huckleberry Point serves almost as a mirror to the nearby Codfish Point (Guide #17)—indeed, both hikes start from the same trailhead, and they offer two unique perspectives over Platte Clove and the Hudson Valley below. Both, too, are relatively simple and unchallenging trails that can be tackled by hikers of all skill levels. As with Codfish Point, one could also visit the Upper Platte Clove Waterfall (Guide #16) in addition to this hike, just a short walk from the parking area.

GETTING THERE

Take Exit 20 (Saugerties) off the New York State Thruway for NY-32, then turn left to head west on NY-212. Continue on NY-212 West for 2.3 miles, then make a slight right onto Blue Mountain Road. In another 1.4 miles, turn left onto West Saugerties Road/NY-33. Drive for 3 miles before continuing straight onto Platte Clove Road. The road ascends steeply, with winding turns and incredible views of the clove to your left. This road is closed seasonally, and be wary of driving conditions in periods of inclement weather. Parking can be found on either side of the road by the trailhead.

GPS SHORTCUT

Direct your GPS to navigate you to "Huckleberry Point," and it should take you to the appropriate parking area.

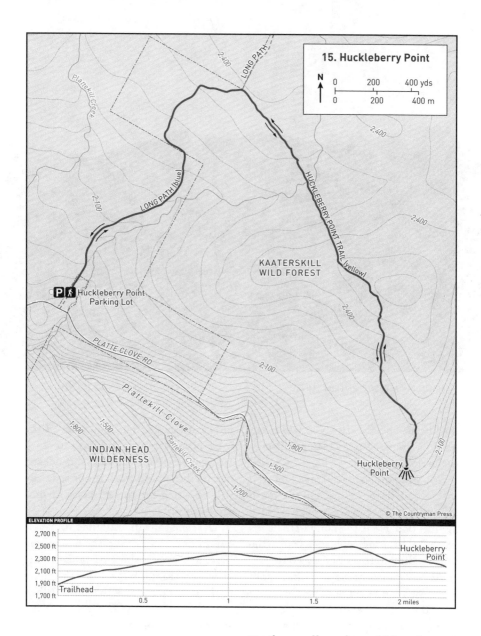

THE TRAIL

The DEC parking area is about a hundred feet off the main road, with the trail register next to a metal gate and the trailhead. Sign in at the register and continue past the gate, heading north up a rocky jeep trail.

Follow the blue blazes of the Long Trail as well as the red-blazed snowmobile trail. The trail begins with a moderate incline at once, then levels out to a more gradual grade after a quarter mile.

After 0.6 miles, you will reach a V intersection. A sign affixed to a trail at the center of the V points you toward the trail to the right. Veer right, following

LOOKING SOUTH ACROSS PLATTEKILL CLOVE

the blazes. Shortly after, you will reach a second intersection. Once again, stay to the right.

You will now be hiking on a foot trail with a moderate incline. Only a tenth of a mile later, you will reach a third intersection. Here, the Long Path heads north. Take the yellow-blazed trail to the right leading to Huckleberry Point.

At 1.3 miles, cross a small, quiet creek on a land bridge of stones. Soon after, the trail will begin to ascend more steeply. You will crest the hill around mile marker 1.7, the high point of the hike. From here it is downhill to reach Huckleberry Point—though this doesn't mean all the hard work is done, as you will have to make this climb in reverse on the return journey.

Descend the hill until the trail levels out around 2 miles into the hike. From here, it is only a short distance to the viewpoint. At the ledge, enjoy the views to the east and across the clove. When you are ready to return, retrace your steps back to the parking area.

16

Upper Platte Clove Waterfall

DISTANCE: 1 mile

TYPE: Out and back

DIFFICULTY: Easy

HIKING TIME: 0.5 hours

While not as grand as Kaaterskill Falls (Guide #12) to the northeast, the Upper Platte Clove Waterfall offers a very similar hike to a more obscure reward. The beautiful waterfall scene at the end of both hikes is accessible after only half a mile of easy trail. But similar to Kaaterskill Falls, these falls can still pose some dangers. Here, at the upper end of the dramatic Platte Clove, potentially fatal risks await hikers who wander off-trail or attempt this hike during times when there are unsafe conditions. This hike should never be attempted on days when the trail may be wet or icy, as much of the hike cuts across a steep bank with only a narrow strip of sure footing, and a fall from the wrong spot on the trail might easily prove deadly. It's best to turn to another destination if there has just been a heavy rainfall to wash out the trail, but in normal conditions, you'll find an underappreciated gem at the end of this short, pleasant stroll.

GETTING THERE

Take Exit 20 (Saugerties) off the New York State Thruway for NY-32, then turn left to head west on NY-212. Continue on NY-212 West for 2.3 miles, then make a slight right onto Blue Mountain Road. In another 1.4 miles, turn left onto West Saugerties Road/NY-33. Drive for 3 miles before continuing straight onto Platte Clove Road. The road ascends steeply, with winding turns and incredible views of the clove to your left. This road is closed seasonally. Even when it is open, travelers should be wary of driving conditions in periods of inclement weather. Parking can be found on either side of the road by the trailhead.

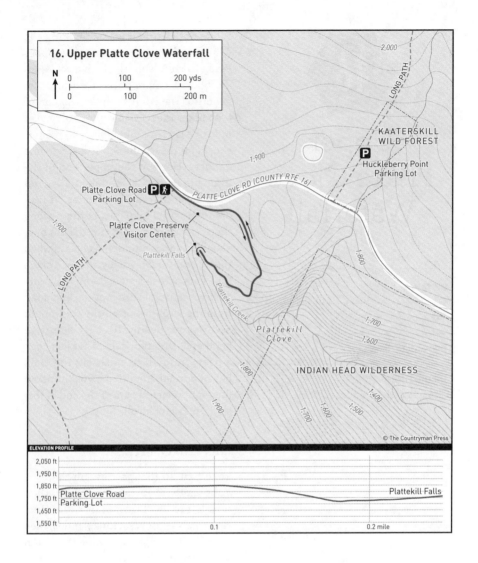

16. Upper Platte Clove Waterfall

N

| 0 | 100 | 200 yds |
| 0 | 100 | 200 m |

2,000

LONG PATH

KAATERSKILL
WILD FOREST

1,900

Huckleberry Point
Parking Lot

Platte Clove Road
Parking Lot

PLATTE CLOVE RD (COUNTY RTE 16)

1,900

Platte Clove Preserve
Visitor Center

Plattekill Falls

LONG PATH

1,800

Plattekill Creek

Plattekill
Clove

1,700

1,600

1,800

INDIAN HEAD WILDERNESS

1,400

1,900

1,700

1,600

1,500

© The Countryman Press

ELEVATION PROFILE

| 2,050 ft |
| 1,950 ft |
| 1,850 ft |
| 1,750 ft | Platte Clove Road | Plattekill Falls |
| 1,650 ft | Parking Lot |
| 1,550 ft |

0.1   0.2 mile

GPS SHORTCUT

Type "Devils Kitchen, Hunter, NY" into Google Maps and your GPS will navigate you to the appropriate trailhead.

THE TRAIL

To begin the hike, exit the parking lot on Platte Clove Road following the aqua blazes of the Long Path. (If you parked in the larger lot by the Huckleberry Point trailhead, you will have to walk to the Platte Clove Road lot before starting the hike.) Just ahead, you will see a red cabin on the left in the Platte Clove Preserve. This is the home of the Artist-in-Residence program run by the Catskill Center, and between the house and the road above you will find a trail leading down into the clove.

After a few hundred feet of trails sloping slowly downhill, you will come to a plaque covering the history of the clove, with views of Platte Clove glimpsed through the trees. Here, the trail cuts

PLATTE CLOVE WATERFALL

to the right and begins to descend more steeply.

Continue as the narrow, occasionally precarious trail follows a ledge cut into the canyon wall. The narrow trail will begin to descend more quickly as it cuts through the clove toward the falls, sometimes dropping steeply down earth thick with tree roots.

Soon, the trail will end at the base of the 70-foot Plattekill Falls. Be especially careful around the base of the falls, as the flat ground and shallow stream look benign enough, but footing on the rocks can be more precarious than it would seem to be.

When you are ready, retrace your steps to return to your car.

Codfish Point from Platte Clove

DISTANCE: 4 miles

TYPE: Out and back

TOTAL ELEVATION GAIN: 650 feet

MAXIMUM ELEVATION: 2,500 feet

DIFFICULTY: Easy

HIKING TIME: 2 hours

The eastern sections of the Catskill Park running parallel to the Hudson River boast some of the most memorable vistas in the range—as evidenced by the heavy focus on this area by the early tourism and hotel industry. Here, just north of the site of the former Overlook Mountain House, a series of cloves and ridgelines drops off severely into the valley below, creating ideal viewpoints at numerous spots. On a clear day, the entire Hudson Valley spreads out before you, with views beyond to the Shawangunk Ridge, the Berkshire Mountains of Massachusetts, and even to the Green Mountains of southern Vermont. Codfish Point delivers on a number of these views, and its rewards are accessible to just about any level of hiker, as this 4-mile round-trip hike poses few difficulties.

Further adding to the appeal of this hike, handmade stone furniture can be found at various points of the trail, presenting unique opportunities for photo ops and rest spots (though for a more intense experience with the mysterious furniture, one should visit Dibble's Quarry, Guide #21). More adventurous hikers can choose to extend this hike to Echo Lake (for a total distance of 8.8 miles) or even to the Overlook Mountain House and fire tower (a total of 13 miles). For an easier add-on, the Upper Platte Clove Waterfall (Guide #16) is available from the same parking area and is a very short hike.

GETTING THERE

Take Exit 20 (Saugerties) off the New York State Thruway for NY-32, then turn left to head west on NY-212. Continue on NY-212 West for 2.3 miles, then make a slight right onto Blue Mountain Road. In another 1.4 miles, turn left onto West Saugerties Road/NY-33. Drive for 3 miles

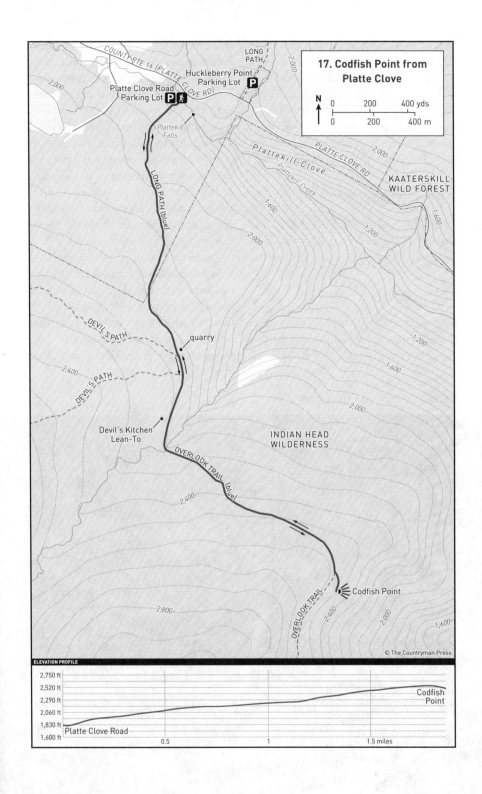

17. Codfish Point from Platte Clove

N

0   200   400 yds
0   200   400 m

COUNTY-RTE 16 (PLATTE CLOVE RD)

LONG PATH

Huckleberry Point Parking Lot

Platte Clove Road Parking Lot

Plattekill Falls

LONG PATH (blue)

Plattekill Clove

Plattekill Creek

PLATTE CLOVE RD

KAATERSKILL WILD FOREST

DEVIL'S PATH

quarry

DEVIL'S PATH

Devil's Kitchen Lean-To

OVERLOOK TRAIL (blue)

INDIAN HEAD WILDERNESS

Codfish Point

OVERLOOK TRAIL

© The Countryman Press

ELEVATION PROFILE

2,750 ft			
2,520 ft			Codfish Point
2,290 ft			
2,060 ft			
1,830 ft			
1,600 ft	Platte Clove Road		
	0.5	1	1.5 miles

before continuing straight onto Platte Clove Road. The road ascends steeply, with winding turns and incredible views of the clove to your left. This road is closed seasonally, so be wary of driving conditions in periods of inclement weather. Parking can be found on either side of the road by the trailhead.

GPS SHORTCUT

Type "Devils Kitchen, Hunter, NY" into Google Maps and your GPS will navigate you to the appropriate trailhead.

THE TRAIL

Start south on the Long Path and immediately cross the small wooden bridge spanning the Plattekill Creek. The trail will be marked with aqua-colored Long Path markers as well as the blue diamond blazes of the Platte Clove Preserve.

Follow a shady path heavily knotted with thick tree roots. A little under a mile from the trailhead, you will reach a rocky area to the left of the path, where makeshift seats and benches have been crafted from stone slabs. The bluestone of this wild furniture originated from the old quarry at the site, but these days, the clearing makes for the perfect place to stop, relax, and enjoy a snack.

Immediately after the quarry, the trail will reach a sharp fork and the trail markers will change to the blue DEC blazes. First, hike past the red-blazed Devil's Path trail as it veers to your right, and then almost immediately after, continue straight again as the Long Path

FOOTBRIDGE SPANNING PLATTEKILL CLOVE

RUSTIC BLUESTONE QUARRY SEATING

and the southern loop of the Devil's Path trail join, heading west toward Indian Head Mountain.

Following the blue markers, you will soon reach the Devil's Kitchen Lean-To. While its perch just off the path and near an idyllic stream makes it another perfect spot for taking a break, not to mention camping, you'll have company on most days. Even arriving early in the afternoon, you can expect at least one group of campers to have already staked out a spot. Few hikes in the eastern Catskills are particularly obscure, and thus snagging a prime camping spot during much of the year can be a challenge.

Just after the lean-to, you will reach another bridge. Soon after crossing this stream, the trail will begin to climb slightly. These trails are part of a network of old carriage roads that once allowed visitors to access the Overlook Mountain House, only a few miles to the south (and still accessible via this same trail, as an extended hike).

Tackle this moderate ascent for another 0.75 mile. Shortly before reaching Codfish Point, the trail will level off, and you will spot a cairn marking the yellow-blazed spur trail to your left. Follow this side path for a short distance to reach Codfish Point.

At the overlook, find another of the stone-slab chairs created for you to perch on, and enjoy the sweeping views of the river valley. Facing the east, with an easy, short trail (and a nearby lean-to), Codfish Point makes for an excellent spot to catch the sunrise.

When you are ready to return, retrace your steps to your car.

Platte Clove offers an easily accessible bonus if you're still looking to explore after your venture to Codfish Point. See the Guide (#16) for the Upper Platte Clove Waterfall to extend your hike and visit the falls, only a short walk from the parking area.

Overlook Mountain

DISTANCE: 4.6 miles

TYPE: Out and back

TOTAL ELEVATION GAIN: 1,380 feet

MAXIMUM ELEVATION: 3,140 feet

DIFFICULTY: Strenuous

HIKING TIME: 3.5 hours

Overlook Mountain is known less for the exciting nature of its trails than for the history waiting at its top. At the southeast edge of the range, just to the north of the town of Woodstock, the mountain played a major part in the Catskills' status as a tourism destination for wealthy New Yorkers during the past century. While the route up is a plain yet grueling old carriage road making a steep, straight ascent, the rewards are worth it. The fire tower here is one of only five remaining in the Catskills (the others can be found on Hunter Mountain, Balsam Lake Mountain, Red Hill, and Tremper Mountain). Nearby, more history lurks in the woods: The former site of the Overlook Mountain House can be explored just off the trail.

The site of the former hotel is one of the few lasting reminders of the grand mountainside structures that once lured wealthy vacationers up into the mountains. The Overlook Mountain House opened in 1871, with a capacity for 300 guests and the highest elevation of any hotel in the area, at 2,920 feet. The business had several lives, as fire destroyed the structure in 1887 and again in 1923. Then-owner Morris Newgold hired architect Frank P. Amato to redesign and rebuild the hotel, but its final incarnation was ultimately never finished. The hotel's elevation and lack of access to rail transportation made the site difficult to reach, and this ultimately thwarted plans for the hotel's rebirth. Eventually, the project was abandoned due to financial difficulties, and the hotel was boarded up for good in 1940 after the land was acquired by the State of New York.

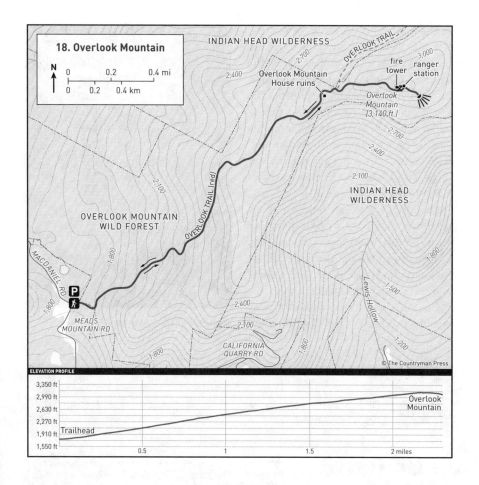

18. Overlook Mountain

INDIAN HEAD WILDERNESS

OVERLOOK TRAIL

N
0   0.2   0.4 mi
0   0.2   0.4 km

2,400   Overlook Mountain
         House ruins

fire
tower   ranger
         station
3,000

Overlook
Mountain
(3,140 ft.)

2,700

2,400

OVERLOOK MOUNTAIN
WILD FOREST

OVERLOOK TRAIL (red)

2,100

INDIAN HEAD
WILDERNESS

2,100

1,800

1,800

MACDANIEL RD

1,800

P

MEADS
MOUNTAIN RD

2,400

2,100

1,800

CALIFORNIA
QUARRY RD

Lewis Hollow

1,500

1,200

1,800

© The Countryman Press

ELEVATION PROFILE

3,350 ft
2,990 ft
2,630 ft
2,270 ft
1,910 ft Trailhead
1,550 ft

Overlook
Mountain

0.5   1   1.5   2 miles

GETTING THERE

Take Exit 19 (Kingston) from the New York State Thruway. Keep right onto NY-28 West, then continue west on NY-28 for 6 miles. Turn right onto NY-375 North. After 3 miles, turn left onto Mill Hill Road, then continue through the town of Woodstock. From the center of Woodstock, take Rock City Road north. Rock City Road will turn into Meads Mountain Road after half a mile. Continue another 2 miles along winding mountain roads to the trailhead. The parking lot is large, but this is a very popular hike near a bustling tourist town, and the lot can easily fill up on weekends.

GPS SHORTCUT

Type "Overlook Mountain" into Google Maps and your GPS will navigate you to the appropriate trailhead.

THE TRAIL

The trail to the top of Overlook Mountain, following a well-graded gravel path, is incredibly easy to follow. In fact, this really isn't a trail so much as an actual road, albeit a very grueling and unrelenting one.

At 1.25 miles in, you will encounter a branch where a side trail loops into private property. Stay left to continue on the main trail and walk for another half mile. Before reaching the top of the mountain, you will spot the ruins of the Overlook Mountain House in the woods. Be very careful when exploring the woods around the structures, as timber rattlesnakes are known to frequent this area. They are commonly seen around the road near the ruins and the summit both. The ruins themselves are, of course, very dilapidated.

Though the hotel has been out of use for almost a century, its past glory can still be felt over the sprawl of the complex. A large guesthouse still stands behind the Mountain House itself, with a stone pool that served as the water supply.

Continuing on from the ruins, 2 miles from the trailhead, you will encounter a

OVERLOOK MOUNTAIN FIRE TOWER

THE RUINS OF OVERLOOK MOUNTAIN HOUSE

LOOKING EAST FROM THE TOWER ON OVERLOOK MOUNTAIN

to the east, leading to an excellent view of the southeast.

The 60-foot tower is the newest of those remaining in the Catskills. While the Overlook Mountain tower has only been at its present location since 1950, the tower was actually moved from its original location on Gallis Hill, near Kingston. It was built there in 1927. From the top, you will be able to enjoy breathtaking views of the Hudson River, Ashokan Reservoir, Indian Head Mountain Range, and West Kill Mountain.

Return along the same route back to the trailhead.

Indian Head Mountain Loop

DISTANCE: 6.25 miles

TYPE: Loop

TOTAL ELEVATION GAIN: 1,570 feet

MAXIMUM ELEVATION: 3,573 feet

DIFFICULTY: Very Difficult

HIKING TIME: 4.5 hours

Indian Head Mountain is named for its triad of peaks, which, when viewed from the north or east, seem to form a face. The mountain is the easternmost of the six major peaks on the Devil's Path hiking trail, and this infamous trail section, known for its high level of difficulty, creates unique obstacles. A popular day hike despite its difficulty, the loop of Indian Head Mountain throws hikers into one of the most challenging sections of the Devil's Path.

The ominous name of the trail—as well as other nearby landmarks, like the Devil's Tombstone and Devil's Kitchen—originated from the early superstitious Dutch settlers, fearful of what might lurk in these then-mysterious mountains. The settlers believed that the Catskills harbored the Devil himself, and the jagged contours of the Devil's Path specifically were fashioned in such a way that only the Devil would be able to climb them. Of course, maybe those settlers were really just bitter about being out of shape. The deep valleys in between the peaks of the Devil's Path are what make this trail so challenging—traversing from east to west, a hiker will endure more than 14,000 feet of elevation change over roughly 25 miles.

GETTING THERE

Take Exit 20 (Saugerties) from the New York State Thruway, then turn left onto NY-212/NY-32. At the traffic light, take a right onto NY-32 North. In 6 miles, continue straight onto NY-32A. In 1.9 miles, turn left onto Route 23A and drive up the winding mountain road toward Tannersville. At the traffic light in Tannersville, take a left onto NY-16/Platte Clove Road. Continue south for 6 miles, then turn right onto Prediger Road. After half

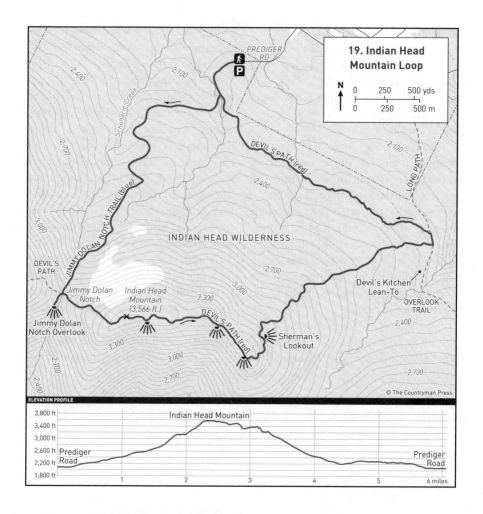

19. Indian Head Mountain Loop

N ↑

0   250   500 yds
0   250   500 m

DEVIL'S PATH (red)

LONG PATH

JIMMY DOLAN NOTCH TRAIL (blue)

Schoharie Creek

INDIAN HEAD WILDERNESS

DEVIL'S PATH

Jimmy Dolan Notch   Indian Head Mountain (3,566 ft.)

Jimmy Dolan Notch Overlook

DEVIL'S PATH (red)

Sherman's Lookout

Devil's Kitchen Lean-To

OVERLOOK TRAIL

© The Countryman Press

ELEVATION PROFILE

	Indian Head Mountain	
3,800 ft		
3,400 ft		
3,000 ft		
2,600 ft Prediger		Prediger
2,200 ft Road		Road
1,800 ft		

1   2   3   4   5   6 miles

---

a mile, the road will become dirt. Take the dirt road to the DEC parking area.

GPS SHORTCUT

Type "Prediger Road Trail Head" into Google Maps and your GPS will navigate you to the appropriate trailhead.

THE TRAIL

From the parking area, find the sign identifying the various destinations accessible from the Devil's Path trailhead. Follow the red blazes for about a quarter mile. Turn right to follow the blue-blazed Jimmy Dolan Notch Trail.

The grade will start level but grow increasingly steeper as you hike. Follow the blue blazes for 1.5 miles. When there are no leaves on the trees, you might spot Kaaterskill High Peak and Round Top Mountain behind you through the forest canopy.

Just under 2 miles from the trailhead, you will reach Jimmy Dolan Notch and another trail junction. Heading straight will take you on a short side trail to a viewpoint. Take the side trail, and enjoy the views looking south toward Woodstock before returning to the intersection. From the blue blazes of the Jimmy Dolan Notch Trail, make a left onto the Devil's Path trail (a right if you are returning from the viewpoint). Head east, following the red blazes of the Devil's Path trail.

The Devil's Path is infamous as one of the most challenging sections of trail in the northeastern United States, with countless obstacles of every kind throwing themselves in your way as you tackle the path's steep climbs. The remaining trail from the Jimmy Dolan Notch to the Indian Head summit is only half a mile, but it climbs another 500 feet in elevation. Be especially wary of slick, wet stones or loose rocks.

Hike through a forest of hemlock and balsam fir. Nearing the summit, the trail will suddenly flatten, and this will be the only indication that you have reached the peak. There are no views from the summit of Indian Head.

Descending from the summit, you will face some of the most challenging portions of the Devil's Path. First up is a rock chimney that requires hikers to worm their way down between the two rock faces. After this, you will descend a large stone wall that is most easily navigated using the thick tree roots that weave up and down its surface. Using the roots to hold on to, climb down this rock face with extreme care.

At mile 3, you will reach a high overlook facing east with a stunning view of the Hudson, the Ashokan Reservoir, Overlook Mountain, and even distant ranges beyond: the Shawangunks by New Paltz, and the Taconics and Berkshires in Massachusetts. Several ledges

THE SCENIC EASTERN SHOULDER OF INDIAN HEAD MOUNTAIN

ON THE TRAIL TO THE SUMMIT OF INDIAN HEAD

on this section of the trail offer stunning, sweeping views to the south and the east.

Continue following the red blazes. After about 1.25 miles, you will reach an intersection with the blue-blazed Overlook Trail, an easy carriage road leading toward the Devil's Kitchen Lean-To and Codfish Point. Take a sharp left to stay on the Devil's Path trail. Follow the trail for another 1.5 miles before coming to another junction. You have now completed the loop. Stay straight, following the red blazes still, to return to the parking area on Prediger Road. Do you feel like you wrestled with the Devil today?

Twin Mountain

DISTANCE: 5.8 miles

TYPE: Out and back

TOTAL ELEVATION GAIN: 1,590 feet

MAXIMUM ELEVATION: 3,640 feet

DIFFICULTY: Strenuous

HIKING TIME: 4 hours

Twin Mountain gets its name from the dual high points on the summit, both of them over 3,500 feet. Although they are separated by more than half a mile, the elevation does not drop far enough between the two for them to be considered distinct peaks. Located along the famous Devil's Path range, this hike is quite challenging. However, those who are willing to put in the effort are rewarded with fantastic panoramic views of the surrounding mountains, some of the best in the Catskill Park. During colder months, the trail can become very slippery with ice and snow. If you plan to hike in these conditions, be sure to have sturdy traction devices. Even so, be prepared for the eventuality that you may have to abandon your hike if the trail is too unsafe. The climb to the summit can turn dangerous even when conditions are favorable.

GETTING THERE

Take Exit 20 (Saugerties) from the New York State Thruway, then turn left onto NY-212/NY-32. At the traffic light, take a right onto NY-32 North. In 6 miles, continue straight onto NY-32A. In 1.9 miles, turn left onto Route 23A, and drive up the winding mountain road toward Tannersville. At the traffic light in Tannersville, take a left onto NY-16/ Platte Clove Road. Continue south for 6 miles, then turn right onto Prediger Road. Follow Prediger Road until it ends. You will find the parking area at the end of the road.

GPS SHORTCUT

Searching for "Twin Mountain" may cause your GPS to navigate you to an alternate trailhead. Input "Prediger Road Trail Head" into Google Maps for

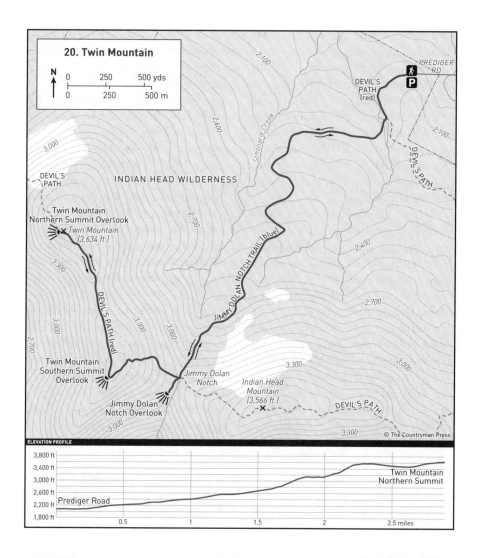

20. Twin Mountain

N
0 — 250 — 500 yds
0 — 250 — 500 m

RREDIGER RD

DEVIL'S PATH (red)

DEVIL'S PATH

Schoharie Creek

INDIAN HEAD WILDERNESS

DEVIL'S PATH

2,100

2,400

3,000

2,700

2,400

2,700

Twin Mountain Northern Summit Overlook

Twin Mountain (3,634 ft.)

JIMMY DOLAN NOTCH TRAIL (blue)

3,300

DEVIL'S PATH (red)

3,000

3,300

3,000

2,700

Twin Mountain Southern Summit Overlook

Jimmy Dolan Notch

Indian Head Mountain (3,566 ft.)

3,300

3,000

Jimmy Dolan Notch Overlook

DEVIL'S PATH

3,300

3,000

© The Countryman Press

ELEVATION PROFILE

3,800 ft
3,400 ft
3,000 ft
2,600 ft
2,200 ft
1,800 ft

Prediger Road

Twin Mountain Northern Summit

0.5 — 1 — 1.5 — 2 — 2.5 miles

your GPS to navigate you to the appropriate trailhead.

THE TRAIL

The hike starts at the beginning of the red-blazed Devil's Path trail. The Devil's Path is widely regarded as the most demanding trail in the Catskill Park, crossing six high peaks while rising and falling more than 15,000 feet over the course of 24 miles. Luckily, on this hike you will only gain about 150 feet of elevation over the course of 0.2 mile before veering right onto the blue-blazed Jimmy Dolan Notch Trail.

Cross a seasonal run immediately after picking up the blue-blazed trail. The trail may be a little muddy at first, depending on conditions, but you should not have a problem crossing. For a mile the trail meanders through serene deciduous forest, weaving gently uphill. There is a stream off the trail to your right about a tenth of a mile away, and the sound of rushing water cascading down the hillside may reach your ears if it is running heavily. The trail is rocky in places, but for now the grade is only slightly steeper than your short jaunt on the Devil's Path. The Jimmy Dolan Notch Trail bypasses 4.25 miles of the Devil's Path that would otherwise send you up and over Indian Head Mountain, a route that would add an additional 500 feet of elevation gain to the already daunting climb ahead of you.

The last half mile of the Jimmy Dolan Notch Trail is very steep, periodically requiring you to use your hands as you scramble up the side of the mountain. Take your time here and exercise caution, as you will ascend approximately 500 feet over just half a mile.

When the trail levels out, you will have reached Jimmy Dolan Notch, the col between Indian Head Mountain and Twin Mountain. The blue blazes end here, and your route rejoins the Devil's Path once again. The notch sits at 3,100 feet above sea level and is a nice place to take a break, as it will be your only reprieve from ascending aggressively until you reach the top. There is a good view a short distance south of the col, on an unmarked but easily discernible herd path. The view may be somewhat obscured by foliage and underbrush, and pales by comparison with the vistas on the summit, but this is still a good place to catch your breath after the intense climb.

Resume climbing, heading westward on the red-blazed Devil's Path. If you went to the viewpoint in the col, turn left onto the trail. If you decided not to visit the viewpoint, you will turn right. Almost immediately after you leave the col, the climbing becomes very aggressive and will stay that way until you reach the summit in 0.4 mile, sending you scrambling up several steep, rocky, rooty areas. You will have to use your hands in many places to advance uphill. This is a good example of what the majority of the Devil's Path is like. Turning around as you ascend will occasion-

SUGARLOAF MOUNTAIN IN THE DISTANCE BEHIND TWIN'S NORTHERN SUMMIT

TWIN'S NORTHERN SUMMIT TOWERING ABOVE DIBBLE'S QUARRY

ally reward you with views of Big Indian Mountain looming to the southwest.

Close to the top, the trail will begin to level, and in a short distance you will come to the vista on Twin's southern summit, an exposed rock ledge with plenty of room for several people. The view here is awe-inspiring, a wide panoramic expanse facing southwest, stretching more than 180 degrees. You will absolutely want to stop here to rest and enjoy the scenery. From here you can see Woodstock, Cooper Lake, and Overlook Mountain to the south. Looking west you will see Sugarloaf and Plateau Mountains in the distance.

When you are finished admiring the view, continue on the Devil's Path heading back into the woods on a narrow trail through a tunnel of conifer trees. The trail will dip slightly between Twin's high points, but for the most part the path is easy to walk, especially compared to the climb up from the notch. In 0.7 mile you will reach Twin's northern summit, which boasts yet another sweeping view. From here you can get a close-up view of Sugarloaf Mountain, which sits along the Devil's Path about 2 miles west of Twin.

To return to your vehicle, turn around and follow the red blazes back the way you came. Be very careful as you climb down to the col, as the descent can be just as challenging as the climb up. Turn left onto the Jimmy Dolan Notch Trail when you come to it, and continue descending back to the beginning of the Devil's Path and the parking area. You'll find that the gradual grade you walked earlier is even more enjoyable after the grueling climb and descent you just endured!

21

Dibble's Quarry

DISTANCE: 2 miles	
TYPE: Out and back	
TOTAL ELEVATION GAIN: 340 feet	
MAXIMUM ELEVATION: 2,350 feet	
DIFFICULTY: Easy	
HIKING TIME: 1.5 hours	

As the name would imply, Dibble's Quarry was once mined for bluestone, which was used as a building material in years past. The quarry is no longer operational, but what remains is a sight to behold. Unknown persons working laboriously over the years (or maybe Sasquatch—we shouldn't rule it out) have spent countless hours building makeshift towers, tables, and chairs with the flat, smooth rocks. An excellent expedition for explorers seeking maximum payoff for minimal effort, this easy hike is very attractive to young and old alike, offering sweeping views of the surrounding mountains and the valley below. Dibble's Quarry can be visited on its own, or combined with more strenuous hikes like Twin Mountain (Guide #20) and Sugarloaf Mountain (#22), since the trail beyond the quarry eventually meets with the Devil's Path.

GETTING THERE

Take Exit 20 (Saugerties) from the New York State Thruway, then turn left onto NY-212/NY-32. At the traffic light, take a right onto NY-32 North. In 6 miles, continue straight onto NY-32A. In 1.9 miles, turn left onto Route 23A, and drive up the winding mountain road toward Tannersville. At the traffic light in Tannersville, take a left onto NY-16/Platte Clove Road. Continue south for 5 miles, then turn right onto Dale Lane. Follow Dale Lane for 1.2 miles. The parking area is just before Dale Lane becomes Roaring Kill Road.

GPS SHORTCUT

Type "Roaring Kill" into Google Maps and your GPS will navigate you to the appropriate trailhead.

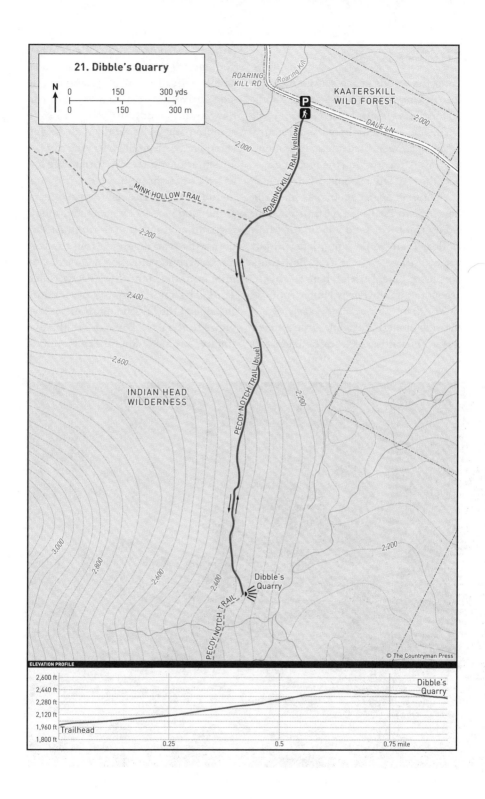

21. Dibble's Quarry

N

| 0 | 150 | 300 yds |
| 0 | 150 | 300 m |

ROARING KILL RD

Roaring Kill

KAATERSKILL WILD FOREST

DALE LN

2,000

2,000

ROARING KILL TRAIL (yellow)

MINK HOLLOW TRAIL

2,200

2,400

2,600

PECOY NOTCH TRAIL (blue)

2,200

INDIAN HEAD WILDERNESS

3,000

2,800

2,600

2,400

Dibble's Quarry

2,200

PECOY NOTCH TRAIL

© The Countryman Press

ELEVATION PROFILE

			Dibble's Quarry
2,600 ft			
2,440 ft			
2,280 ft			
2,120 ft			
1,960 ft	Trailhead		
1,800 ft			
	0.25	0.5	0.75 mile

THE TRAIL

Enter the woods at the southern end of the parking lot and begin an easy walk up the rooty, yellow-blazed Roaring Kill Trail. The trail climbs very gradually, crossing two seasonal streambeds along the way. After crossing the second creek bed, the trail will become a little rockier as the forest opens up. In 0.25 mile, the Roaring Kill Trail ends at a trail junction. Going right will send you on the Mink Hollow Trail, while going left will put you on the Pecoy Notch Trail. Both trails are blazed blue. Turn left here and begin ascending up the Pecoy Notch Trail.

The trail climbs moderately along the side of a hill, through serene mixed forest. You will pass several boulders and large rocky ledges as you continue. When you start to level off, you will notice some small chairs made out of stone along the side of the trail. At times this area can be wet and muddy, but there are solid stepping-stones lining the path, so you should have no problem staying dry.

The trail will start to turn to the left as you pass through a large grove of hemlock trees. Descend over a small stone ledge on rocky steps and follow the trail as it cuts to the right. At this point, the trail emerges from the tree cover, arriving at Dibble's Quarry 0.75 mile from the start of the Pecoy Notch Trail. The quarry area is perched on the side of the hill and offers expansive views to the east. You can see the distinctive profile of Round Top Mountain

SCENIC VIEWS OF KAATERSKILL HIGH PEAK FROM DIBBLE'S QUARRY

THE BLUESTONE THRONE ROOM

and Kaaterskill High Peak to your left, and the northwestern summit of Twin Mountain to your right, with the Platte Clove Valley spreading out into the distance between the two. You will want to set aside a good amount of time to explore this area. There are little stony trails leading all over the quarry, to man-made walls and fences.

Perhaps the highlight of the quarry is a medieval-looking court up a short staircase, complete with two thrones made out of bluestone. There are several other chairs in the area as well, making this a perfect place for a picnic. Early risers would find a real treat in watching the sunrise from here, and they might even catch a fleeting glimpse through the trees of the giant, humanoid cryptids that may or may not have constructed this mysterious place. These sites of stone furniture are truly one of the oddest and most

delightful quirks of Catskills hiking—a trailside feature you won't encounter very many other places in the country.

Up the trail a short distance, there are a few more man-made stone structures, but the real highlight is the throne room. When you are finished enjoying the quarry, retrace your footsteps back to the parking lot. Keep an eye out for large, barefooted footprints in the mud that you certainly did not make—and, indeed, no human could have.

If you continue following the Pecoy Notch Trail, you will eventually cross a stream just above a waterfall, and further on from there, you will reach a beaver pond that gives you good views of Pecoy Notch, which sits between Twin Mountain and Sugarloaf Mountain. The blue blazes end a mile uphill from the quarry, where the trail meets with the red-blazed Devil's Path.

Sugarloaf Mountain Loop

DISTANCE: 7 miles

TYPE: Loop

TOTAL ELEVATION GAIN: 1,760 feet

MAXIMUM ELEVATION: 3,810 feet

DIFFICULTY: Very difficult

HIKING TIME: 5.5 hours

While Sugarloaf Mountain boasts no views from its own summit, ledges just below and around the peak of the park's thirteenth-highest mountain offer their own stunning views. Two quarries and unique stone furniture fashioned by previous hikers add to this exciting day hike, though it is a challenging one. Sections of both the ascent and descent can be extremely difficult, so this hike may not be one to tackle when the trail will be wet, or in winter, unless one is fully prepared for the challenge with the proper equipment.

If you have ever wondered why there are so many mountains and hills named Sugarloaf—at least four within a two-hour drive of the Catskills, and over two hundred such prominences in just the United States—these landforms are named after an antiquated method of packaging sugar. Until the late nineteenth century, a sugarloaf was refined sugar processed into the shape of a rounded cone; this was the easiest and most common method for distributing sugar. Sugarloaves came in a variety of sizes, but generally, the larger the loaf, the lower the grade of sugar. Strangely, the conical shape of a sugarloaf does not particularly resemble most of these mountains—in New York, especially, the mountains and hills tend to be low and sprawling due to age, while a sugarloaf is tall and narrow, shaped vaguely like a missile.

GETTING THERE

Take Exit 20 (Saugerties) from the New York State Thruway, then turn left onto NY-212/NY-32. At the traffic light, take a right onto NY-32 North. In 6 miles, continue straight onto NY-32A. In 1.9 miles, turn left onto Route 23A, and

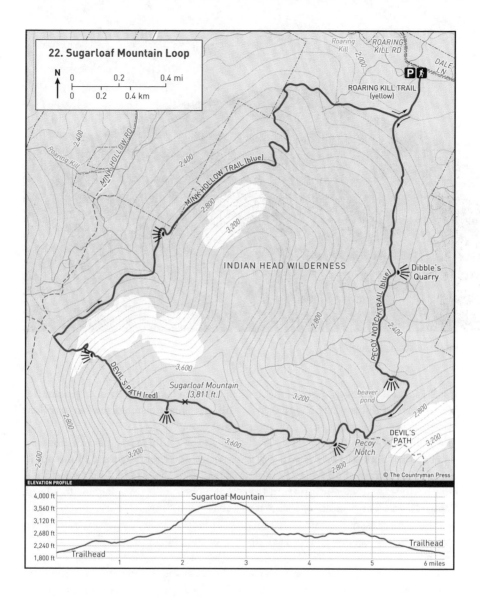

22. Sugarloaf Mountain Loop

N

0   0.2   0.4 mi

0   0.2   0.4 km

Roaring Kill

ROARING KILL RD

DALE LN

ROARING KILL TRAIL (yellow)

MINK HOLLOW RD

Roaring Kill

MINK HOLLOW TRAIL (blue)

2,400

2,800

3,200

INDIAN HEAD WILDERNESS

Dibble's Quarry

PECOY NOTCH TRAIL (blue)

2,800

2,400

DEVIL'S PATH (red)

Sugarloaf Mountain (3,811 ft.)

3,600

3,200

beaver pond

2,800

DEVIL'S PATH

3,200

2,800

2,400

3,200

3,600

Pecoy Notch

2,800

© The Countryman Press

ELEVATION PROFILE

4,000 ft		Sugarloaf Mountain				
3,560 ft						
3,120 ft						
2,680 ft						
2,240 ft					Trailhead	
1,800 ft	Trailhead					
	1	2	3	4	5	6 miles

drive up the winding mountain road toward Tannersville. At the traffic light in Tannersville, take a left onto NY-16/ Platte Clove Road. Continue south for 5 miles, then turn right onto Dale Lane. Continue another 0.75 mile to the DEC parking lot on the left side of the road.

GPS SHORTCUT

Type "Roaring Kill" into Google Maps and your GPS will navigate you to the appropriate trailhead.

THE TRAIL

From the parking area on Dale Lane, follow the yellow blazes of the Roar-

PROFILE OF SUGARLOAF MOUNTAIN

ing Kill Trail to the registration box at the start of the trail. You will arrive at a trail junction after only a quarter of a mile. Here, the Pecoy Notch Trail meets the Mink Hollow Trail, both using blue blazes. Sugarloaf is most commonly hiked ascending from the Pecoy Notch Trail, making a shorter but more aggressive ascent. Turn left and follow the Pecoy Notch Trail to begin the loop.

The trail will begin to climb with a moderate grade. Very shortly, you'll spot the remnants of an old bluestone quarry by the trail. Soon, you will see stone chairs along the trail, constructed out of stones from the old quarry. The trail descends slightly to a north-facing viewpoint over Round Top Mountain and Kaaterskill High Peak. At about 0.9 mile, you will arrive at an area where many of these elaborate stone chairs, along with other assorted furniture,

have been fashioned by entrepreneurial hikers. This area makes for an excellent rest stop.

At the 1-mile mark, the trail crosses a stream and then begins to climb uphill parallel to the stream. Just under half a mile beyond, you will come to a large beaver pond. Twin Mountain and Sugarloaf Mountain are both visible, looming over the pond.

At mile 1.75, you will arrive at Pecoy Notch, at a junction with the red-blazed Devil's Path trail. Turn right onto the Devil's Path. The trail will almost immediately begin a steep ascent of Sugarloaf Mountain. The Devil's Path is known for its difficulty, and the next half-mile of trail is a good demonstration of why. Extra caution is advised for this stretch.

Shortly after the 2-mile mark, you will spot a side trail leading to a viewpoint. After the challenging ascent up the Devil's Path, this is an excellent opportunity to take a breather. The trail from this point is much easier. After you pass the sign indicating you have reached 3,500 feet in elevation, the trail will alternate between level sections and moderate climbs.

The summit of Sugarloaf Mountain is flat and, unfortunately, offers no views. However, only a few hundred feet beyond, a yellow-blazed trail on the left will lead you to a ledge looking out to the south. Here, you can see as far as the Ashokan Reservoir in the distance.

Continue down the Devil's Path trail as the descent becomes gradually steeper. While not as severe as the steep ascent up the mountain, the trail here can be difficult, as it is frequently wet and slick. Navigate this section—about a mile long, descending 1,000 feet—with caution. Despite its challenges, the rock formations here also offer dramatic visu-als, with large cliff-like overhangs and stacked ledges forming natural stone tunnels.

After about a mile, you will come to a trail junction with the blue-blazed Mink Hollow Trail. Turn right onto the Mink Hollow Trail to complete the loop and return to your car. The trail will remain relatively level as it follows, then crosses, streams for the next half-mile.

A short while later, the trail will briefly climb once again before reaching a ledge with a view out to Mink Hollow and Plateau Mountain beyond. From here, continue on a woods road, past a second, less memorable quarry. After the quarry, the grade will be relatively level. Soon you will arrive at the junction where you began the loop. Turn left to follow the yellow blazes of the Roaring Kill Trail back to the parking area.

VIEW OF TWIN MOUNTAIN'S DUAL SUMMITS FROM SUGARLOAF MOUNTAIN

Plateau Mountain from Warner Creek

DISTANCE: 8.5 miles

TYPE: Out and back

TOTAL ELEVATION GAIN: 2,340 feet

MAXIMUM ELEVATION: 3,840 feet

DIFFICULTY: Strenuous

HIKING TIME: 5 hours

While this route to the summit of Plateau Mountain is more than 2 miles longer than the trail from Devil's Tombstone, you'll likely find it to be a much more manageable ascent. This is due to the fact that you'll climb more steadily over the course of 3.5 miles, as opposed to the 1,600 feet climbed in 1.3 miles on the Devil's Path route. That isn't to say that this hike is easy, since this trailhead is roughly 500 feet lower than the one at Devil's Tombstone. There are tradeoffs as well. The Warner Creek Trail doesn't have the large, open vistas that the Devil's Path offers, but you'll still be able to catch views from smaller, slightly more obstructed points on the trail. And because it is a longer hike, it's usually not as busy, so you have a better chance of enjoying these views in solitude.

GETTING THERE

From the New York State Thruway, take Exit 19 (Kingston) and pick up NY-28 heading west. Follow NY-28 West for 22.6 miles, and turn right onto Main Street in Phoenicia. Turn left onto NY-214 in 0.2 mile, immediately after crossing a bridge spanning Stony Clove Creek. Continue on NY-214 heading north, and in 8 miles turn right onto Notch Inn Road. Park on the wide shoulders of the road, a few hundred feet before a bridge crosses a tributary of Stony Clove Creek.

GPS SHORTCUT

Type "Notch Inn Road" into Google Maps, and your GPS will navigate you to the appropriate trailhead.

THE TRAIL

From the trailhead, begin walking up Notch Inn Road. You will cross the afore-

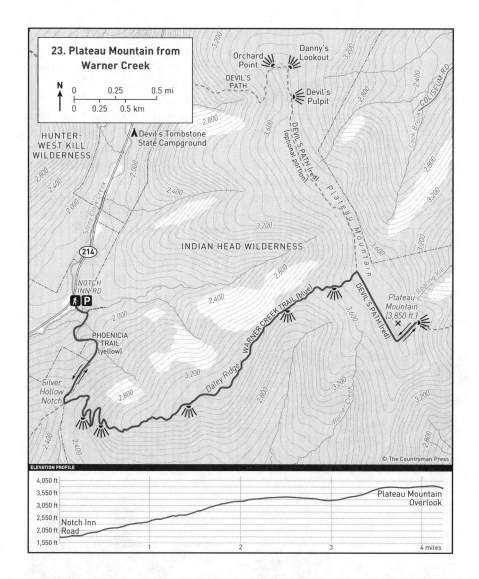

23. Plateau Mountain from Warner Creek

ELEVATION PROFILE

mentioned bridge and proceed to road-walk uphill for 0.4 mile. Just before the road ends at a private residence, veer left onto a yellow-blazed trail leading into the woods. The trail follows a rocky old forest road, continuing uphill. Follow this abandoned road and in half a mile you will arrive at Silver Hollow Notch, the col between Edgewood Mountain on your right and Daley Ridge on your left. The yellow blazes end here, at the junction of the Warner Creek Trail.

Turn left and follow the blue trail markers of the Warner Creek Trail. In 0.2 mile you will begin to ascend steeply through a series of rocky switchbacks, which will send you up nearly 700 vertical feet. There are some pleasant views of the valley below through the trees as you make your way up. Eventually, the trail will begin to level off as you reach the top of Daley Ridge. For the next mile the trail is much less intense, gently meandering over the mellow crest of the ridge, followed by a gradual descent of about 100 feet.

The last leg of the climb continues to follow the blue blazes going straight up a steep shoulder of the mountain. There are two very good vistas along this trail, leading off to the right on obvious herd paths. These areas are small rock ledges on the rim of the ridge. From these points, you can see Little Rocky Mountain and Olderhark Mountain to the south, across a massive tree-covered bowl. Drainage from the southern flank of Plateau Mountain forms the headwaters of Warner Creek, which eventually joins with Stony Clove Creek north of Phoenicia. Take your time as you ascend and be sure to enjoy these pristine viewpoints.

After 3 miles of hiking on the Warner Creek Trail, you will reach the ridge of Plateau Mountain, shrouded in dense evergreen trees. Turn right here onto a narrow, tunnellike trail, and continue on the red-blazed Devil's Path for half a mile. At this point you are on the true high point of Plateau. There are no views from here, but if you continue on the Devil's Path, descending for about a tenth of a mile, you will reach a viewpoint atop a large boulder. From here you can see Sugarloaf Mountain to the east, as well as the Platte Clove Valley.

VIEW FROM PLATEAU MOUNTAIN LOOKING EAST TOWARD SUGARLOAF

When you are ready to leave, turn around and head back to the junction of the Warner Creek Trail. Turn left and follow the path back to the yellow-blazed trail. Turn right, follow the yellow blazes, and roadwalk the last portion of the hike back to your vehicle.

There are additional views on the western side of the Plateau ridge, should you wish to extend your hike. To visit these viewpoints, continue to follow the Devil's Path west, instead of turning left onto the Warner Creek Trail after visiting the true summit. You will reach the furthest vista in 1.7 miles from the turnoff for the Warner Creek Trail. From these areas you can see Hunter Mountain, Southwest Hunter Mountain (Leavitt Peak), Kaaterskill High Peak, and the Blackhead Range in the distance. Return to the junction of the Warner Creek Trail and follow it to get back to the parking area. The hike from the trail junction traverses the Plateau ridge and is easy walking, though it will add 3.4 miles to your total mileage, making for a fairly intense outing, all told.

LOOKING WEST TOWARD PLATEAU MOUNTAIN FROM THE MINK HOLLOW TRAIL

Plateau Mountain from Devil's Tombstone

DISTANCE: 6 miles	
TYPE: Out and back	
TOTAL ELEVATION GAIN: 1,840 feet	
MAXIMUM ELEVATION: 3,840 feet	
DIFFICULTY: Strenuous	
HIKING TIME: 4 hours	

True to its name, Plateau Mountain's level summit is a pleasure to hike, as you ridge walk the length of the mountain. Getting to the top is no easy feat, however, as the ascent follows the Devil's Path seemingly straight up for the majority of the hike, gaining almost 2,000 feet of elevation. That being said, the trail is very pretty, especially in the fall when the leaves are changing color, setting the hills ablaze in a spectacular show. Devil's Tombstone State Campground is located at the base of the mountain and is open May through September, making it possible to turn a day hike into a weekend base-camp adventure. While not the easiest way to reach the summit, the route described here is the most direct and offers more in the way of vistas than other options do. If you're planning to hike Plateau Mountain in the winter, the trailhead on Notch Inn Road (Guide #23) offers a more mellow ascent, although traction devices are still highly recommended.

GETTING THERE

Take Exit 20 (Saugerties) from the New York State Thruway, then turn left onto NY-212/NY-32. At the traffic light, take a right onto NY-32 North. In 6 miles, continue straight onto NY-32A. In 1.9 miles turn left onto Route 23A, and drive up the winding mountain road toward Tannersville. From Tannersville, continue another 2.5 miles on NY-23A until you reach the intersection with NY-214. Take a left onto NY-214 South and continue for 3 miles. The parking area will be on your right, just after passing Notch Lake.

GPS SHORTCUT

Type "Notch Lake" into Google Maps and your GPS will navigate you to the appropriate trailhead.

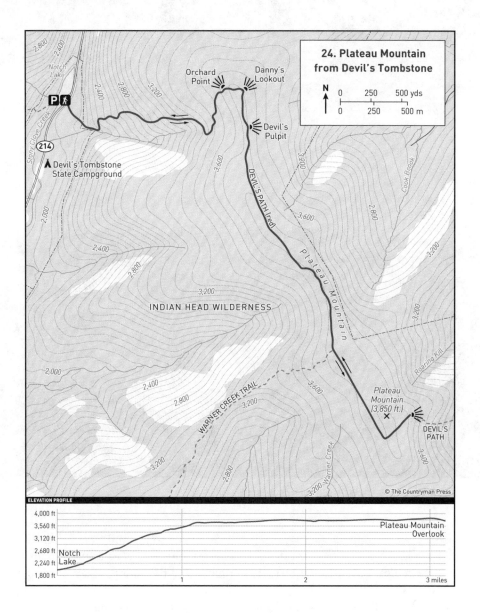

24. Plateau Mountain
from Devil's Tombstone

N

| 0 | 250 | 500 yds |
| 0 | 250 | 500 m |

Notch Lake

Orchard Point

Danny's Lookout

Devil's Pulpit

DEVIL'S PATH (red)

Stony Clove Creek

214

Devil's Tombstone State Campground

Cook Brook

Plateau Mountain

INDIAN HEAD WILDERNESS

WARNER CREEK TRAIL

Roaring Kill

Plateau Mountain (3,850 ft.)
×

DEVIL'S PATH

Warner Creek

© The Countryman Press

ELEVATION PROFILE

4,000 ft
3,560 ft
3,120 ft
2,680 ft
2,240 ft Notch Lake
1,800 ft

Plateau Mountain Overlook

1   2   3 miles

THE TRAIL

From the parking area, cross the road and head into the woods on a short staircase cut into the side of the hill. This is the Devil's Path, a 24-mile red-blazed trail that spans the length of the mountain range, crossing six peaks over 3,500 feet in elevation along the way. You will stay on this trail for the entirety of your hike. Follow the red blazes for about a tenth of a mile, gaining elevation moderately, before coming to a bend in the trail next to the stream to your right. Descending to the stream, you can see small cascades further uphill.

Continue following the Devil's Path and begin hiking uphill on a very steep grade. For the next 1.2 miles, this incline will take you relentlessly upward, climb-

VIEW OF THE BLACKHEAD RANGE FROM PLATEAU MOUNTAIN

ing 1,450 feet in the process. The hillside to the right of the trail drops off sharply into the valley below. In autumn, the climb can be especially tricky, as leaves on the trail will make it slippery and you will be unable to see the rocky path underneath, adding an element of surprise to each step. To make the climb more manageable, there are stone steps on certain portions, and short switchbacks occasionally, but neither of these will likely do much to distract you from the fact that the trail is very, very steep. What else did you expect of a hike that started out by the Devil's Tombstone?

Take your time, and remember to enjoy the mountain (you're having fun, right?). You will know you are through the worst of it when the trail begins to bend to the right, edging the rim of a ravine. Continuing on, you will make an abrupt left turn and start to ascend much more gently than before.

A quarter of a mile from the turn, you will reach an easily surmountable stone ledge. The trail goes up the ledge, bringing you to your first vista, at Orchard Point, which rewards you for your climb with excellent views of the Stony Clove area below. Hunter Mountain and Southwest Hunter Mountain (sometimes called Leavitt Peak) dominate the view to the northwest. The viewing area is fairly large and can accommodate a few groups of hikers.

When you are ready to resume your hike, keep following the Devil's Path as the trail levels out, becoming much easier to walk. At this point you are essentially on the Plateau ridge and will climb infrequently and only moderately to reach the true summit on the southern tip of the mountain. Roughly a quarter of a mile from Orchard Point lies the second viewpoint of the day at Danny's Lookout. While not as expansive as the previous vista, Danny's Lookout gives you an entirely different perspective, as it faces northeast. Easily identifiable Kaaterskill High Peak and Round Top Mountain are visible to the east, and off in the distance to the north lies the Blackhead Range. A little way beyond Danny's Lookout is another viewpoint, although it is mostly overgrown. You may be able to catch a glimpse of Sugarloaf Mountain from here, but there is a much better view of Sugarloaf near the true summit.

Continue to follow the red blazes along the ridge of the mountain, through densely wooded evergreen forest. You will feel like you are walking through a tunnel as the trees make this portion of the trail dark, peaceful, and somewhat narrow. In 1.7 miles from Orchard Point, the trail will meet with the Warner Creek Trail on your right. Stay on the Devil's Path, and in half a mile, you will reach the true summit of Plateau Mountain. There isn't much to see from this point, but a little further on, about a tenth of a mile, you can catch a good view of Sugarloaf Mountain and the Platte Clove Valley to the east. To reach this vista, continue following the trail, as it turns to your left and descends about 100 feet of elevation, until you reach a small viewing area atop a large, flat boulder.

When you are finished taking in the sights, turn around and retrace your steps along the ridgeline and descend to your car at Notch Lake.

Southwest Hunter Mountain (Leavitt Peak)

DISTANCE: 6.2 miles	
TYPE: Out and back (bushwack required)	
TOTAL ELEVATION GAIN: 1,640 feet	
MAXIMUM ELEVATION: 3,740 feet	
DIFFICULTY: Difficult	
HIKING TIME: 4 hours	

Also known as Leavitt Peak, in honor of the first finishers of the Catskill 3500 challenge, Southwest Hunter Mountain sits along an unmarked spur trail off of the Devil's Path. While there are no views from the summit, the route described here is arguably the most scenic, leading you past a pleasant waterfall and a small vista on the way. The last mile to the peak is on an unmarked herd path, with a short, easy bushwhack at the very end. You will have to stay alert to reach the top! Southwest Hunter Mountain can be climbed on its own or in conjunction with Hunter Mountain. There are several ways to access the start of the herd path. The hike described here, while not the shortest, climbs the least amount of elevation of any route to the start of the unmarked trail.

GETTING THERE

From the New York State Thruway, take Exit 19 (Kingston) and head west on NY-28. Continue about 28 miles to the junction with NY-42 in Shandaken. Proceed north on NY-42 for 7.4 miles to the hamlet of West Kill, then turn right. Follow Spruceton Road (County Route 6) for another 6.7 miles, past a dead end sign, to a large parking area for Hunter Mountain on the left side of the road. If this parking lot is full, there are two more lots further down the road.

GPS SHORTCUT

The nearest searchable location is Spruceton Inn in West Kill, NY. Search Google Maps for "Spruceton Inn," and when you arrive, continue to head east on Spruceton Road for approximately 2 miles to reach the trailhead.

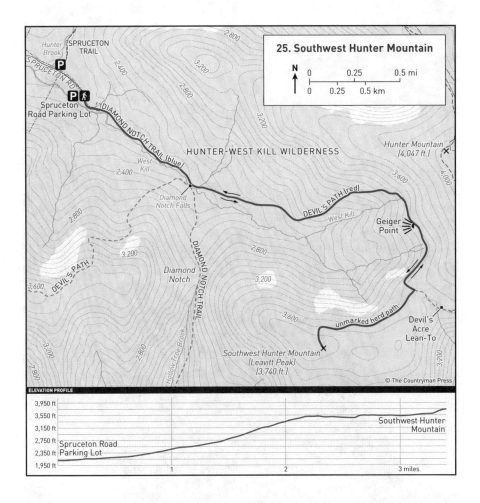

THE TRAIL

From the parking area, enter the woods at the end of Spruceton Road and begin walking a rocky horse trail alongside West Kill. This is the Diamond Notch Trail, a blue-blazed multiuse trail that will intersect with the Devil's Path in 0.7 miles. The trail ascends moderately, passing a gate soon after you enter the woods. Continue to follow the blue trail markers until you come to an intersection in a large grassy clearing. Diamond Notch Falls are located to your right and are well worth exploring. The Diamond Notch Trail crosses the creek above the falls and continues south to a shelter, descending on an old road grade further on. The red-blazed Devil's Path bisects the Diamond Notch Trail, heading across the falls to your right before turning to the west toward West Kill Mountain. From the grassy clearing, go straight, heading east on the Devil's Path.

The Devil's Path climbs slightly more aggressively immediately after leaving the trail intersection, and the trail is much rockier than before. You will have to be careful of your footing as you walk this stretch of the trail, since some of the rocks are loose and can easily cause you to sprain your ankle. After about

DIAMOND NOTCH FALLS

0.6 mile of relatively easy climbing, the trail bends to the left and starts heading uphill through open forest on a steep grade that is just as rocky. Take your time as you ascend. In the spring and summer, this climb can be wet from runoff and overgrown with stinging nettles. It is recommended that you wear pants or long socks to protect against these pesky plants.

Toward the top of the climb, you will see an unmarked herd path that leads off to the right. Following this short trail for a few feet will take you to Geiger Point, a small rock ledge that offers terrific views looking out over Diamond Notch Hollow below. Southwest Hunter Mountain will be to your left, and West Kill Mountain is located to your right. Return to the main trail to resume your hike. In a short distance from the vista, the trail levels off significantly. As before, you may experience soupy, muddy sections on this leg of the hike. Continue to follow the Devil's Path through hemlock, balsam, and birch forest.

Half a mile from Geiger Point you will come to an obvious, unmarked herd path leaving the Devil's Path on the right side of the trail. If you reach the Devil's Acre Shelter, then you have gone too far and will have to turn around. Turn onto this unmarked trail, and follow it for roughly 0.75 mile. The grade is easy, as it walks an old gravel railroad bed, through dense conifer forest.

Toward the end of the railroad grade, you will come to a small cairn marking a narrow path leading uphill to your left. This junction can be easy to miss, so stay alert. Head uphill on the narrow path, climbing 140 feet over a tenth of a mile. There may be a decent amount of blowdown along this narrow, overgrown trail, but it is still fairly easy to follow. At the end of this path you will reach the summit of Southwest Hunter Mountain, 3,740 feet above sea level, fenced in by thick vegetation. A canister bolted to a tree marks the summit. Sign into the logbook in the canister if you wish, and return to the old railroad grade the way you came.

From the railroad grade, turn right and head back to the Devil's Path. Turn left and follow the red markers downhill, back to Diamond Falls and the junction with the blue-blazed trail. Retrace your previous course along this trail, arriving at the parking area and your vehicle, where the Diamond Notch Trail ends.

CASCADING RAPIDS, DIAMOND NOTCH FALLS

26

Hunter Mountain

DISTANCE: 8.2 miles

TYPE: Loop

TOTAL ELEVATION GAIN: 1,900 feet

MAXIMUM ELEVATION: 4,045 feet

DIFFICULTY: Strenuous

HIKING TIME: 6 hours

Hunter Mountain is well known as a ski resort and festival destination, popular with crowds seeking beer, music, or slopes. In spite of its status as the second-highest peak in the Catskills and its renown as the cultural hub of the region, Hunter does not receive quite the attention Slide Mountain receives as a hiking destination. Nonetheless, it is a fantastic choice for a challenging day hike, with a unique state fire tower: the highest-elevation fire tower in all of New York State.

GETTING THERE

From the New York State Thruway, take Exit 19 (Kingston) and head west on NY-28. Continue about 28 miles to the junction with NY-42 in Shandaken. Proceed north on NY-42 for 7.4 miles to the hamlet of West Kill, then turn right. Follow Spruceton Road (County Route 6) for another 6.7 miles, past a dead end sign, to a large parking area for Hunter Mountain on the left side of the road. If this parking lot is full, there are two more lots further down the road.

GPS SHORTCUT

The nearest searchable location is Spruceton Inn in West Kill, NY. Search Google Maps for "Spruceton Inn," and when you arrive, continue to head east on Spruceton Road for approximately 2 miles to reach the trailhead.

THE TRAIL

From the first parking area, cross the steel road barrier and follow the blue-blazed Spruceton Trail northward. Stop at the trail register, about 50 feet up the trail, and register your hike before continuing on the wide, relatively level trail.

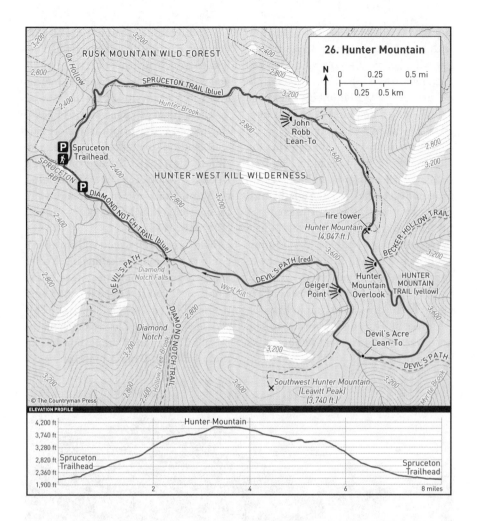

RUSK MOUNTAIN WILD FOREST

SPRUCETON TRAIL (blue)

Hunter Brook

Ox Hollow

John
Robb
Lean-To

Spruceton
Trailhead

SPRUCETON RD

HUNTER-WEST KILL WILDERNESS

DIAMOND NOTCH TRAIL (blue)

fire tower
Hunter Mountain
(4,047 ft.)

BECKER HOLLOW TRAIL

DEVIL'S PATH

Diamond
Notch Falls

DEVIL'S PATH (red)

West Kill

Geiger
Point

Hunter
Mountain
Overlook

HUNTER
MOUNTAIN
TRAIL (yellow)

Diamond
Notch

DIAMOND NOTCH TRAIL

Hollow Tree Brook

Devil's Acre
Lean-To

DEVIL'S PATH

Southwest Hunter Mountain
(Leavitt Peak)
(3,740 ft.)

Myrtle Brook

© The Countryman Press

ELEVATION PROFILE

	Hunter Mountain	
4,200 ft		
3,740 ft		
3,280 ft		
2,820 ft Spruceton		Spruceton
2,360 ft Trailhead		Trailhead
1,900 ft		

2   4   6   8 miles

After about half a mile, you will enter the Ox Hollow area and cross over Hunter Brook on a wide wooden bridge. The trail makes a sharp right turn and begins to ascend gradually.

The broad, steady trail—originally built to allow vehicles access to the fire tower—will continue for about 1.5 miles before veering briefly to the north. Here you will reach a junction. The wide vehicle access road continues straight, heading north down the mountain toward the town of Hunter. To the left is a bushwhacking trail ascending East Rusk Mountain. Turn right to follow the blue-blazed trail, which will continue eastward. The trail will now be rougher, with a much steeper incline.

In a little less than half a mile, you will pass a water source. If needed, follow the sign to the spring, which falls on a side trail leading to the John Robb Lean-To. The lean-to itself is notable for its remarkable views over the Spruceton Valley, making this an excellent spot to pause to rest. At this point you have already climbed to about 3,300 feet in elevation, having ascended some 1,400 feet from the parking lot—so a break is by now well-earned!

Continuing on the blue trail once

again, you will soon come to a junction with the Colonel's Chair Trail, to your left. This yellow-blazed trail brings you to the ski lifts of the Hunter Mountain ski area. (Hunter Mountain also runs a Skyride through most of the summer and early fall at select times.)

Continue straight, still following the blue blazes for another mile. The trail will level off for a time before picking up a moderate incline once again, until you at last reach the large clearing at the summit of the mountain. While there are no views from the summit itself, here you will find the fire tower and the fire observer's cabin.

On a clear day, the fire tower offers views in all directions, including the ski area of Hunter Mountain to the north and the Blackhead Range peaks to the northeast.

When you are ready to make your descent, continue again down the blue-blazed trail. In another quarter of a mile you will reach a four-way trail junction and the former site of the fire tower. To the left, a trail descends to Becker Hollow, and to the right is a short side trail leading to a ledge with an exceptional view over Spruceton Valley. Upon returning to the intersection after enjoying these views, turn right and follow the yellow blazes of the Hunter Mountain Trail.

The forest around you will shift from conifers to maples, oaks, and birch trees as you descend. Continue for a mile and a half until you reach the junction with the red-blazed Devil's Path trail. This trail leads to Stony Clove Notch and the Devil's Tombstone Campground. Continue straight. Only a tenth of a mile

THE RANGER CABIN, FROM THE FIRE TOWER

HUNTER MOUNTAIN FIRE TOWER

after the junction, you will spot the Devil's Acre Lean-To on the right side of the trail.

Continuing on the red-blazed trail, cross a seasonal stream and continue for about half a mile on a relaxed, albeit often wet stretch of trail. The next intersection offers yet another short detour to new viewpoints. Taking the side trail left will bring you to Geiger Point, a rock ledge overlooking Diamond Notch.

After the viewpoint, continue

VIEW LOOKING EAST FROM THE HUNTER MOUNTAIN FIRE TOWER

straight and hike for another mile and a half as the trail descends steadily. After crossing another seasonal stream, you will reach a trail junction in a grassy clearing. The Devil's Path trail turns left to cross the West Kill, but you should follow the blue-blazed Diamond Notch Trail to continue straight ahead. Soon you will pass the Diamond Notch Falls.

Continue until you spot the trail register and reach Spruceton Road. You will have to walk along the road for a quarter mile to reach the DEC parking areas.

West Kill Mountain

The Buck Ridge Lookout, just below the summit of West Kill Mountain, is a favorite of many Catskill hikers. With dramatic views to the south, it is considered one of the best vistas in the Catskill range. The Devil's Path route up West Kill Mountain isn't as challenging as those of some similar hikes, though that's of course a relative comparison—this is still a very strenuous hike.

DISTANCE: 6.4 miles

TYPE: Out and back

TOTAL ELEVATION GAIN: 1,780 feet

MAXIMUM ELEVATION: 3,890 feet

DIFFICULTY: Difficult

HIKING TIME: 4.5 hours

GETTING THERE

From the New York State Thruway, take Exit 19 (Kingston) and head west on NY-28. Continue about 28 miles to the junction with NY-42 in Shandaken. Proceed north on NY-42 for 7.4 miles to the hamlet of West Kill, then turn right. Follow Spruceton Road (County Route 6) for another 6.7 miles, past a dead end sign, to a large parking area for Hunter Mountain on the left side of the road. If this parking lot is full, there are two more lots further down the road.

GPS SHORTCUT

The nearest searchable location is Spruceton Inn in West Kill, NY. Search Google Maps for "Spruceton Inn," and when you arrive, continue to head east on Spruceton Road for approximately 2 miles to reach the trailhead.

THE TRAIL

Walk to the trailhead at the easternmost parking area (if parked in this lot, you will already be right at the trail). Pass the gate at the trailhead and begin hiking on the blue-blazed Diamond Notch Trail. About 100 feet beyond the gate, you will cross over a creek. Continue, following the blue blazes.

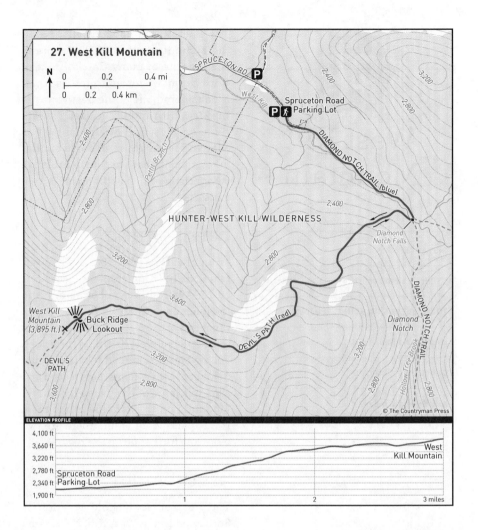

After 0.7 mile, you will arrive at a trail junction. Take the trail to the right, passing by Diamond Notch Falls before heading to the summit of West Kill Mountain, as well as toward Diamond Notch. The Diamond Notch Trail follows the path of an old road that once ran from Spruceton Road to Lanesville, cutting through Diamond Notch Hollow. Taking the red-blazed Devil's Path trail straight would lead you to Hunter Mountain.

Cross over the creek and resume walking the blue-blazed trail. Another split occurs only a few hundred feet after the first junction. Here, the old carriage road heads toward Diamond Notch. Take a right once again, to follow the red blazes west.

The trail begins a steep uphill ascent. Continue for another 2 miles. As the woods transition into a conifer forest, the trail will begin to level off. Eventually you will reach the first of two viewpoints. The first, on the left side of the trail, is the Buck Ridge Lookout. A massive drop-off below the ledge creates an even more dramatic view. A

TAKING A BREAK AT BUCK RIDGE LOOKOUT

LOOKING EASTWARD FROM THE SUMMIT OF WEST KILL MOUNTAIN

second ledge offers views from the other side of the trail, looking roughly north, only a short way beyond Buck Ridge. This ledge looks out over the Spruceton Valley.

The summit of West Kill Mountain is only a short distance beyond. When you are ready to return, retrace your steps to your car.

Tremper Mountain

DISTANCE: 6.1 miles

TYPE: Out and back

TOTAL ELEVATION GAIN: 1,960 feet

MAXIMUM ELEVATION: 2,725 feet

DIFFICULTY: Moderate

HIKING TIME: 3.5 hours

While Tremper Mountain lacks the elevation of many of the Catskills' most dramatic peaks, it was an important home of industry in the nineteenth century. A railroad connecting Tremper Mountain to the Hudson River towns allowed for a succession of enterprises in the area, and the early thriving barkpeeling industry around the mountain eventually gave way to tourism. In the late 1800s, the mountain became the site of the Tremper House, an early railroad resort that proved to be immensely popular, praised for its views by such patrons as Oscar Wilde. Though other hotels in the region were built to boast of their dramatic mountaintop views, the Tremper House was built in a valley, a decision Wilde found more aesthetically appealing, since in valleys "the picturesque and beautiful is ever before you."

After the hotel eventually closed and burned down, the State of New York began buying up land around the mountain to create hiking trails. The 47-foot fire tower at the mountain's summit was built in 1916, though it later closed down in the '60s due to a wildfire. One of the five fire towers remaining in the Catskills, it is joined by the towers on Overlook Mountain, Hunter Mountain, Red Hill, and Balsam Lake Mountain. After the wildfire, the tower on Tremper Mountain was not restored until the end of the century. In 2001, the tower was added to the National Register of Historic Places and reopened to the public.

GETTING THERE

Take Exit 20 (Saugerties) from the New York State Thruway, then turn left onto NY-32 South. Immediately after, continue onto NY-212 at the red light. Drive

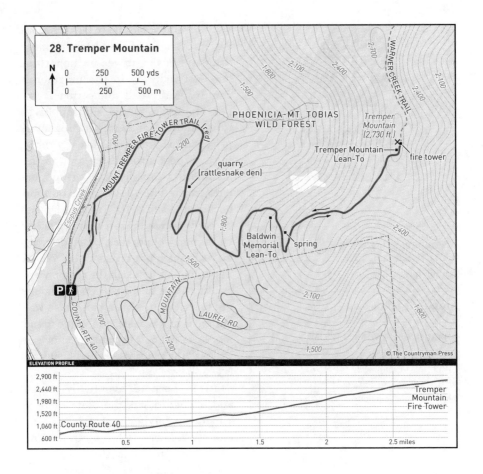

28. Tremper Mountain

PHOENICIA-MT. TOBIAS WILD FOREST

MOUNT TREMPER FIRE TOWER TRAIL (red)

Esopus Creek

WARNER CREEK TRAIL

Tremper Mountain (2,730 ft.)

Tremper Mountain Lean-To

fire tower

quarry (rattlesnake den)

Baldwin Memorial Lean-To

spring

LAUREL RD

COUNTY RTE 40

MOUNTAIN

© The Countryman Press

ELEVATION PROFILE

2,900 ft
2,440 ft
1,980 ft
1,520 ft
1,060 ft County Route 40
600 ft

0.5   1   1.5   2   2.5 miles

Tremper Mountain Fire Tower

for 9 miles until you reach Woodstock, then continue another 1.8 miles to Bearsville. Take a right in Bearsville to stay on NY-212 toward Phoenicia. Continue on NY-212 for 9 more miles before turning right onto County Route 40. Continue another 2 miles; the DEC parking area will be on your right.

GPS SHORTCUT

Type "Tremper Mountain Trail" into Google Maps and your GPS will navigate you to the appropriate trailhead.

THE TRAIL

The trailhead, beginning near the bank of the Esopus Creek, can be found next to the DEC message board. You will cross several wooden bridges before climbing a series of stone steps up a steep hill. Afterward, the trail levels out and meets an old truck path after another quarter mile. Here you will find the DEC registration box where you can register your hike.

As you continue, several streams cross the trail. The trail will again begin to steepen as you ascend the southwestern slope of Mount Tremper. The trail here is often quite slick.

THE DEVIL'S PATH, FROM THE FIRE TOWER ON TREMPER MOUNTAIN

LOOKING SOUTHWEST FROM TREMPER MOUNTAIN

Hike through a series of switch-backs, and a little over 1 mile into the hike, you will spot a bluestone quarry to the left of the trail. Be very careful in this area, as the quarry is known to be home to a timber rattlesnake den. The snakes are especially active on sunny spring days.

The trail continues a steady uphill climb. At the 2-mile mark of the trail, a small side trail heads toward the Baldwin Memorial Lean-To. Just past the lean-to is a water source, with a sign on the right side of the trail pointing you toward the spring.

At the 3-mile mark, shortly before reaching the summit, you will pass a second lean-to on the left side of the trail. The fire tower is only a few hundred feet beyond. From the top of the tower, hikers can enjoy views of Twin Mountain's summits, Plattekill, Indian Head, Plateau, Hunter, Slide, Wittenberg, and more. On a good day, you will be able to make out the Shawangunks to the south, and even the Hudson Highlands beyond.

When you are ready, return to your car by the same route.

Tanbark Loop

DISTANCE: 2.3 miles

TYPE: Lollipop

TOTAL ELEVATION GAIN: 620 feet

MAXIMUM ELEVATION: 1,440 feet

DIFFICULTY: Moderate

HIKING TIME: 1.5 hours

Conveniently located just off of Main Street in Phoenicia, the Tanbark Trail is an excellent trek for hikers on a time crunch and is a pleasant walk at any time of day. Despite its short length, the Tanbark Trail offers some interesting features for a relatively small amount of effort, including open vistas, towering rock walls, and a look at the economic history of the surrounding area. Be prepared to see a good number of other hikers, as the accessibility and proximity to downtown Phoenicia make this a fairly popular destination that attracts hikers of all skill levels.

The Tanbark Trail is a fantastic hike in summer and in fall at peak foliage, featuring scenic views of the surrounding mountains, the winding Esopus Creek, and the town of Phoenicia itself. There are a few sections of steep climbing, so traction devices (snowshoes, crampons) are recommended for those wishing to enjoy the trail during the winter months.

GETTING THERE

From the New York State Thruway, take Exit 19 (Kingston) and pick up NY-28 heading west. Follow NY-28 West for 23 miles to the town of Phoenicia. At Phoenicia, turn onto Main Street. Travel northeast on Main Street for 0.3 mile, passing Church Street, until you reach Ava Maria Drive on your left. Park on Main Street and walk up Ava Maria Drive for a tenth of a mile and turn right, proceeding to Parish Field. The trailhead is signed, across the field to the right of the playground.

GPS SHORTCUT

Direct your GPS to navigate you to the town of Phoenicia, and follow the above instructions from there.

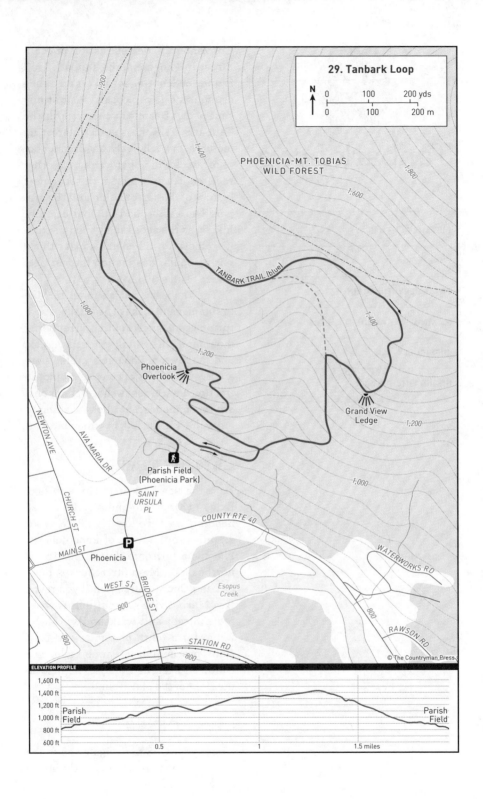

29. Tanbark Loop

N

| 0 | 100 | 200 yds |
| 0 | 100 | 200 m |

1,200

1,400

1,600

1,800

PHOENICIA-MT. TOBIAS
WILD FOREST

TANBARK TRAIL (blue)

1,400

1,000

1,200

Phoenicia
Overlook

Grand View
Ledge

1,200

Parish Field
(Phoenicia Park)

SAINT
URSULA
PL

NEWTON AVE

AVA MARIA DR

CHURCH ST

COUNTY RTE 40

1,000

WATERWORKS RD

P

MAIN ST

Phoenicia

WEST ST

BRIDGE ST

800

Esopus
Creek

800

RAWSON RD

800

STATION RD

800

© The Countryman Press

ELEVATION PROFILE

| 1,600 ft |
| 1,400 ft |
| 1,200 ft |
| 1,000 ft |
| 800 ft |
| 600 ft |

Parish
Field

Parish
Field

0.5   1   1.5 miles

PHOENICIA OVERLOOK ON THE TANBARK LOOP

THE TRAIL

Enter the woods at the edge of Parish Field, and follow the blue-blazed trail across a small run. The path climbs over some medium-sized boulders and ascends for about 100 feet before a hairpin switchback leads to a more moderately graded trail. Be on the lookout for the turn, as it can be easy to miss. From the turn, follow the trail along the foot of a tall, sheer cliff, enjoying the uniquely eroded rock formations and various overhangs.

At 0.3 mile from the trailhead, reach a trail junction. There is a sign that will inform you that the trail is a loop from this point on, and you have the option of going left or right. The trail maintainers suggest going left first, as the climb is slightly more gradual. Turn left and follow the trail, climbing steeply through sparse, open woods. There are several large, craggy boulders scattered along the trail amid shrubby underbrush. This area was mined for bluestone in the 1800s, and some of the quarry is still visible among the trees, although much of it is overgrown. After a short while, the trail levels off as you

ASCENDING THE TANBARK LOOP

reach your first of two viewpoints. The Phoenicia Overlook boasts sweeping views of distant Panther Mountain and the town of Phoenicia nestled quaintly beneath Romer Mountain. A sign features a brief history of the town and its economic importance to the leather tanning industry.

From here the trail climbs slightly before dropping nearly 80 feet in elevation. Pick up an old rocky woods road and begin another steep ascent. The trail momentarily levels off at 1,340 feet before reaching a split. A woods road veers to the right and descends steeply, bypassing a moderate climb before joining the trail again near the second vista. Go left and climb to another quarry area before a rocky descent to Grand View Ledge.

After taking in the view, continue descending on steep, rocky terrain. At roughly 500 feet past Grand View Ledge, the woods road rejoins the trail from the right. Turn left here and follow the blue blazes, dropping 250 feet until you return to the trail junction. At this point, you have finished the loop portion of the trail. Follow the path back along the foot of the rock wall, and return to the trailhead in 0.3 mile.

III.

SOUTHERN

Wittenberg and Cornell Mountains

DISTANCE: 9.4 miles	
TYPE: Out and back	
TOTAL ELEVATION GAIN: 2,480 feet	
MAXIMUM ELEVATION: 3,860 feet	
DIFFICULTY: Strenuous	
HIKING TIME: 6 hours	

Located in the Slide Mountain Wilderness, Cornell and Wittenberg make up the eastern half of the Burroughs Range. From these two mountains, you'll enjoy sweeping views and unique natural rock formations. The ascent is intense, however, so be prepared and make sure you have plenty of time set aside to fully enjoy this hike. Slide Mountain, the tallest peak in the Catskills, sits 2 miles to the west of Cornell and Wittenberg along the same footpath, drawing significant attention to the area, so expect to see a number of people hiking this historic trail as well. This range was named after renowned nature essayist John Burroughs, who was known to frequent these particular mountains.

GETTING THERE

From the New York State Thruway, take Exit 19 (Kingston) and pick up NY-28 heading west. Follow NY-28 West for 23 miles. Half a mile after passing the town of Phoenicia, turn left onto Woodland Valley Road. Woodland Valley Road crosses the Esopus Creek and turns right. Stay on Woodland Valley Road for 4 miles as it bends to the south. The parking area is a large dirt pull-off next to Woodland Valley Campground. It will be on the right side of the road.

GPS SHORTCUT

Type "Woodland Valley Campground, Phoenicia, NY" into Google Maps and your GPS will navigate you to the appropriate trailhead.

THE TRAIL

From the parking area, follow a series of wooden signs that lead you down and across the road a few hundred feet

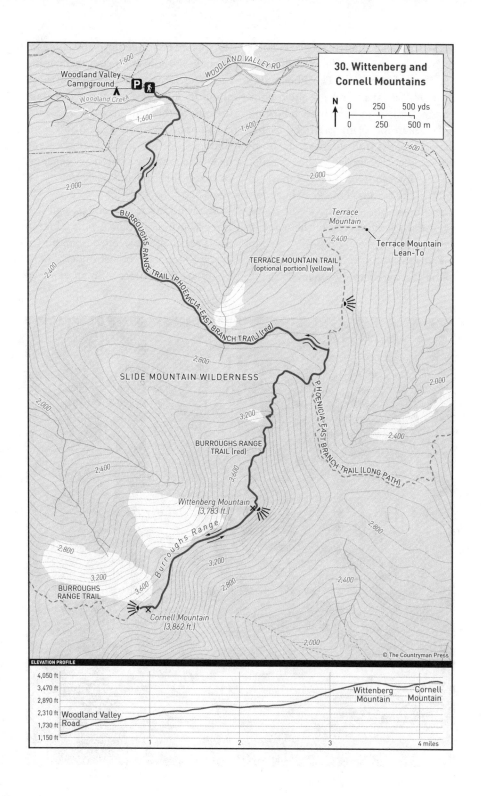

30. Wittenberg and Cornell Mountains

N

| 0 | 250 | 500 yds |
| 0 | 250 | 500 m |

WOODLAND VALLEY RD

Woodland Valley Campground

Woodland Creek

1,600

1,600

1,600

2,000

2,000

1,600

BURROUGHS RANGE TRAIL (PHOENICIA-EAST BRANCH TRAIL) (red)

Terrace Mountain

2,400

Terrace Mountain Lean-To

TERRACE MOUNTAIN TRAIL (optional portion) (yellow)

2,400

2,800

SLIDE MOUNTAIN WILDERNESS

2,000

3,200

PHOENICIA-EAST BRANCH TRAIL (LONG PATH)

2,000

2,400

BURROUGHS RANGE TRAIL (red)

3,600

2,400

Wittenberg Mountain (3,783 ft.)

2,800

Burroughs Range

2,800

BURROUGHS RANGE TRAIL

2,800

3,200

3,200

3,600

2,800

2,400

Cornell Mountain (3,862 ft.)

2,000

© The Countryman Press

ELEVATION PROFILE

| 4,050 ft |
| 3,470 ft |
| 2,890 ft |
| 2,310 ft | Woodland Valley |
| 1,730 ft | Road |
| 1,150 ft |

Wittenberg Mountain   Cornell Mountain

1   2   3   4 miles

to the trailhead. Shortly after you enter the woods, cross the Woodland Creek on a nice footbridge. The Phoenicia–East Branch Trail and the Burroughs Range Trail share tread here, following red markers for 2.8 miles. After crossing the bridge, the trail will ascend, climbing fairly aggressively for about a mile.

Continue to follow the red markers uphill. The trail will make a sharp left turn and begin a much easier grade, eventually leading you to the wooded edge of a very steep drop-off. You can see partial views of Terrace Mountain to the east and the valley below through the trees. The trail follows the ledge for about half a mile before gently bending to the left, cutting across the northern shoulder of the mountain. The path meanders through a peaceful forest, occasionally crossing small streams that cascade downhill. This area can be wet and muddy even in dry seasons, so take your time and place your footsteps carefully.

After hiking for 2.6 miles, you will come to an intersection. A yellow-blazed trail breaks off to the left, descending to Terrace Mountain in just under a mile. There are nice views from an exposed

LIGHT SNOW ON THE WAY TO THE WITTENBERG SUMMIT

THE VIEW FROM CORNELL MOUNTAIN

rocky area about halfway down this trail, as well as a shelter at the very end. Taking a side trip to visit these attractions will add an additional 2 miles to your hike.

Turn right at the trail junction and continue your course along the red-blazed trail. In 0.2 mile of easy walking, the Phoenicia–East Branch Trail breaks off to the left, following blue markers. Ignore this trail, and follow the red blazes uphill. After this point, the trail will begin a very steep ascent, climbing about 1,000 feet up rocky terrain. A number of switchbacks will help you along the way, but you will still have to scramble up many difficult sections over rocks and roots.

When you are near the top, the forest will transition to mostly spruce and balsam fir. The trail will remain very rocky, but the grade will lessen, giving you a chance to catch your breath. Reach the summit of Wittenberg Mountain 1.1 miles after passing the turnoff for the blue-blazed trail. The vista is a long exposed ledge that faces southeast, giving you fantastic views of the Ashokan Reservoir, Ashokan High Point, and other smaller mountains. This is one of the best views in the Catskills, and thus, it is often very busy.

LOOKING SOUTH TO THE ASHOKAN RESEVOIR

You'll want to set aside time to rest here, enjoy a snack, and take in the scenery.

Continue to follow the red blazes, entering the woods at the far end of the vista. The trail will drop in elevation slightly as you come to the col between Cornell Mountain and Wittenberg Mountain, passing some interesting rock formations on the way. The grade is easy here, as you traverse a narrow spine that connects the two peaks through a very enjoyable conifer forest. The trail will begin a moderate ascent toward the summit of Cornell Mountain. You will know you are almost there when you come to a large split in a tall stone ledge. This is known as Cornell Crack, the final obstacle you encounter before reaching the top. You will have to use your hands as you climb this narrow gap, but thankfully the stone is very grippy and makes climbing relatively easy.

A few hundred feet after passing through Cornell Crack, you will reach the summit of Cornell Mountain, 0.8 mile from Wittenberg Mountain. There are obstructed views to the southeast here, as well as better views facing west toward Slide Mountain, Giant Ledge, and Panther Mountain, a short distance past the summit.

When you are ready to leave, retrace your steps to the viewpoint on Wittenberg Mountain and descend back to your vehicle by the way you came. Be extra careful as you go down Cornell Crack, as it may be easier to go up than to go down.

Slide Mountain

DISTANCE: 6.8 miles	
TYPE: Loop	
TOTAL ELEVATION GAIN: 1,750 feet	
MAXIMUM ELEVATION: 4,190 feet	
DIFFICULTY: Strenuous	
HIKING TIME: 4.5 hours	

The highest point in the Catskills, as well as the highest point in the State of New York outside of the Adirondacks High Peaks region, Slide Mountain was in fact not recognized for its prominent station for some time. As hoteliers flocked to build their mountain resorts around the North-South Lake area, Kaaterskill High Peak, at only 3,655 feet, was regarded as the high point in the range for many years.

As the result of long-running quarrels over land rights in the Catskills, no complete, impartial survey was orchestrated until 1886, when the prominence of Slide Mountain was finally becoming noticed. Thanks to the efforts of Princeton geology professor Arnold Henry Guyot, a more extensive survey of the region was conducted, and Slide Mountain was recognized as the highest point in the Catskills, at 4,180 feet.

Slide was named for a landslide in 1819 that scarred the north face of the mountain near its summit. In spite of its height, the hike up Slide Mountain is relatively unchallenging compared to summiting many of the other peaks in the region. However, the view from the summit has been encroached on by trees over the years and thus does not offer quite as dramatic a view as other nearby, lesser mountains. Still, the trail itself is enchanting, making this a pleasurable, surprisingly low-key hike up a mountain rich with history and significance.

GETTING THERE

Take Exit 19 (Kingston) from the New York State Thruway. Turn right onto NY-28 West, then continue west on NY-28 for about 28 miles. At Shandaken, turn right onto NY-42, and in 0.3 mile,

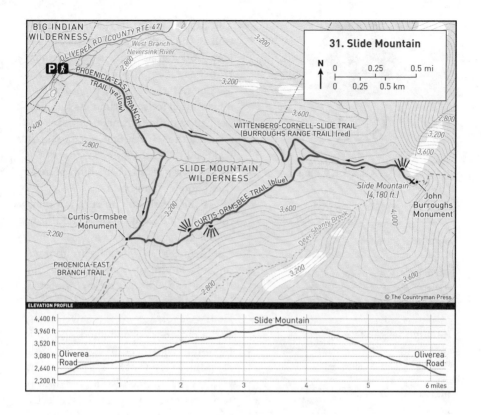

turn left onto Creek Side Drive/Old Route 28. Continue for 2.5 miles, then turn left onto Fire House Road (NY-47). In half a mile, Fire House Road becomes Oliverea Road. Continue for another 10 miles. The parking area is marked by a wooden sign on the left side of the road. While the parking lot is large, accommodating approximately 25 cars, it fills up quickly on weekends due to the popularity of this hike.

GPS SHORTCUT

Type "Slide Mountain Trailhead Parking Lot" into Google Maps and your GPS will navigate you to the appropriate trailhead.

THE TRAIL

The trail starts at the middle of the parking lot near the DEC billboard. Proceed east on the yellow-blazed Phoenicia–East Branch Trail, immediately crossing the west branch of the Neversink River. The water can be difficult to cross after significant rainfall. Following the crossing, you will climb up a rocky footpath, until you ascend a series of stone steps and reach an old woods road in 0.4 mile. Continue to the right.

Follow the yellow-blazed trail along the relatively level woods road. In another third of a mile, you will pass a spring to your left, and shortly after you will come to a junction with the red-blazed Wittenberg-Cornell-Slide Trail, marked by wooden DEC signs. Whichever route you take, you will have the opportunity to return down the other path upon your descent. For this hike, take the path to the right, following the yellow blazes.

After about a third of a mile, at a stream, the trail bends sharply to the right. Around mile marker 1.5, you will come to a second junction. While the yellow-blazed trail that you have been following continues straight, heading south toward Table Mountain, the blue-blazed Curtis-Ormsbee Trail connects to your left. The trail was established by two well-known hikers, William Buckingham Curtis and Allan Ormsbee, who perished in a snowstorm in New Hampshire's Presidential Range in 1900. There is a marble monument at the junction commemorating their legacy. Turn left to follow this trail and the blue blazes.

You will climb a steep but brief section before reaching your first viewpoint, on the left side of the trail, with views to the north and west. A second viewpoint arrives another 0.2 mile up the trail, available from an unmarked side path on the right. Looking south, you will have an excellent view of Table, Lone, Rocky, and Balsam Cap Mountains.

Return to the main trail. Over the next mile, relatively level sections alternate with steeper climbs, before the Curtis-Ormsbee Trail ends at a junction with the red-blazed Cornell-Wittenberg-Slide Trail.

Turn right to continue uphill following the red blazes. Your ascent will grow more severe, and after another three-quarters of a mile, you will arrive at a third viewpoint, and perhaps the best

MEMORIAL PLAQUE ON SLIDE MOUNTAIN SUMMIT

LOOKING SOUTH FROM THE CURTIS ORMSBEE TRAIL

view available from Slide. To the left of the trail, a ledge looks out to panoramic views stretching from Giant Ledge and Panther Mountain, to Woodland Valley, to the Devil's Path to the north.

Shortly after, you will arrive at the summit of Slide Mountain. There, you will find the remains of a fire tower foundation. Unfortunately, there are no views from the summit itself. A short distance further, however, you will come to a large rock ledge that looks out to Cornell and Wittenberg Mountains, though the view has been some-

what blocked by tree cover in recent years. Just below the ledge is a plaque in memory of John Burroughs. Burroughs, a naturalist, essayist, and major figure in the US conservation movement, wrote frequently of his life in the Catskills.

Follow the same route to return down the red-blazed path, until you've reached the junction with the blue-blazed Curtis-Ormsbee Trail. Continue following the red blazes to take the Wittenberg-Cornell-Slide Trail for your descent. Shortly after, the trail bends very sharply to the left, then again to the right. At the first turn, there is an unmarked bushwhacking trail that follows the mountain ridgeline, crossing into private land. This route should not be hiked without permission from the landowner.

The trail here is rocky, but it offers a quick descent. About 1.25 miles after the sharp switchbacks, you will return to the junction with the yellow-blazed Phoenicia–East Branch Trail. You are now only about three-quarters of a mile from the trailhead. Turn right and follow the yellow trail along the old woods road for 0.3 mile, until you come to another intersection with the end of the aforementioned bushwhacking trail. Turn left, and follow the yellow blazes back to the parking area.

Table and Peekamoose Mountains

DISTANCE: 9 miles

TYPE: Out and back

TOTAL ELEVATION GAIN: 1,750 feet

MAXIMUM ELEVATION: 3,845 feet

DIFFICULTY: Strenuous

HIKING TIME: 6 hours

While John Borroughs never commented upon the presence of any moose on the mountain, the famous naturalist was quite fond of the peaceful watershed of the area. The clear waters of the Rondout Creek, a tributary of the Hudson River, are formed on the south and east slopes of Peekamoose and nearby Rocky and Lone Mountains. Burroughs once remarked: "If I were a trout, I should ascend every stream till I found the Rondout." But these mountains will appeal to more than just creek enthusiasts and misguided moose seekers, with an enchanting, mossy spruce fir forest to be wandered along the way, and ample views of the surrounding countryside.

All things considered, this is a hike lovely enough to make up for the disappointingly simple origin of its name: yet another corruption by early settlers of the Native American tongue. Peekamoose is likely no more than a warping of an Algonquin word meaning "broken off smooth."

GETTING THERE

Take NY-55 west until it splits with NY-55A, heading northwest along the north side of the Rondout Reservoir. Drive along the length of the reservoir, until 55A reaches Sundown Road. Turn right onto Sundown Road, then immediately make a left onto Sugarloaf Road. Continue for 4 miles, at which point Sugarloaf Road becomes Red Hill Road and continues straight. Continue for 1.7 miles, then turn left on New Road Hill. After 0.8 mile, turn right onto Denning Road. In another 3.5 miles, you will come to the trailhead where the road ends.

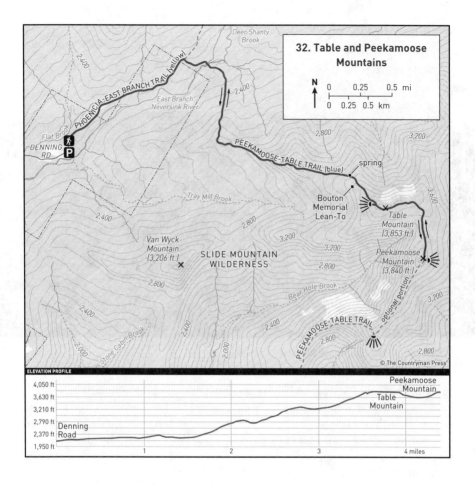

GPS SHORTCUT

Type "Denning Rd. Trailhead" into Google Maps and your GPS will navigate you to the appropriate trailhead.

THE TRAIL

From the parking area, start off on the yellow-blazed Phoenicia-East Branch Trail heading northeast. The trail begins flat, following an old carriage road through conifer forest. Sign in at the trail register, a short distance from the start of the hike. You will notice POSTED signs on the trees during this section of the hike—the land surrounding the trail is private, so be sure to stay on the woods road.

A little after 1 mile, you will reach a well-marked trail junction. Wooden signs indicate the distances to Slide Mountain, Table Mountain, and Peekamoose Mountain, and back to the Denning parking area. Turn right to follow the blue blazes toward Table and Peekamoose mountains.

In another quarter mile, a wooden bridge crosses over the Neversink River. The bridge is sturdy, with wooden railings, but a second bridge crossing shortly after the first one is somewhat

LOOKING NORTH FROM PEEKAMOOSE MOUNTAIN

more precarious. The second bridge is composed of only wooden logs across the water, with no railing.

Continue on the trail as it runs parallel with the water. Soon, you will come to a split in the trail, with a side trail leading off to a campsite. The main trail turns sharply to the right and begins to ascend Table Mountain.

The trail bobs up and down over a series of hills before beginning a more steady ascent. At 2.75 miles, there is a viewpoint through the trees, though foliage may limit the views.

Continue for another half mile past a side trail leading to a spring. Shortly after the spring is a lean-to, a few hundred feet off the main trail.

At 3.5 miles, you will see the marker indicating you have reached 3,500 feet elevation. Only a quarter mile later, you will arrive at a ledge offering a very dramatic view to the west. There is no view

from the top of Table Mountain, so enjoy the horizon here before continuing on to the summit. As you may have guessed (unless you assumed that the mountain was named after more of that strange bluestone mountain furniture), Table Mountain sports a long, flat summit, and it will not feel as if you've reached the peak of a mountain. Continue on the level trail across Table Mountain until the path begins to descend again.

Descend to the col between Table and Peekamoose Mountains. The trail here is relatively easy, and it runs flat in between the two summits before ascending a few hundred feet to the peak of Peekamoose. At 4.5 miles, you will come to the 3,840-foot summit of Peekamoose, with a large boulder denoting the spot on the trail. Only a short distance past the rock, a small side trail to the left of the main path leads to a viewpoint. This vista faces east and

TAKING IN WINTERY VIEWS ON PEEKAMOOSE MOUNTAIN

will give you top-notch views of the surrounding mountainous wilderness.

Continuing to follow the main trail for an additional 0.85 mile will bring you to yet another viewpoint, which faces south. However, this leg of the hike is optional and will add 1.7 miles of hiking to your day.

When you are ready to return, retrace your steps to your car.

Ashokan High Point

DISTANCE: 7.5 miles

TYPE: Out and back

TOTAL ELEVATION GAIN: 1,965 feet

MAXIMUM ELEVATION: 3,090 feet

DIFFICULTY: Moderate

HIKING TIME: 4 hours

This uncrowded hike offers a journey to one of the southernmost viewpoints in the eastern Catskills, overlooking the Ashokan Reservoir just to the east. While an overgrown summit has reduced the potency of the views available from Ashokan High Point, hiking in the late fall or winter still offers a unique, challenging day hike.

GETTING THERE

Take Exit 19 (Kingston) from the New York State Thruway to NY-28 West. Follow NY-28 West for 16 miles. In Boiceville, turn left onto NY-28A/New York City Road and continue another 3 miles. At Peekamoose Road/County Route 42, turn right and drive 4 miles until you arrive at the Kanape Brook parking lot on the right.

GPS SHORTCUT

Typing "Ashokan High Point" into Google Maps will navigate you to a trailhead that is no longer in use—and, in fact, would involve trespassing on private land. Instead, direct your GPS to navigate you to the town of West Shokan and follow the above instructions from there.

THE TRAIL

From the parking area on Peekamoose Road, walk down the road for a short distance to reach the trailhead, indicated by a red trail marker. After only about 100 feet, you will cross a wooden bridge over the Kanape Brook. Shortly after crossing the bridge, sign in at the trail register.

Continue to follow the red blazes as the trail begins with a gentle incline, shadow-

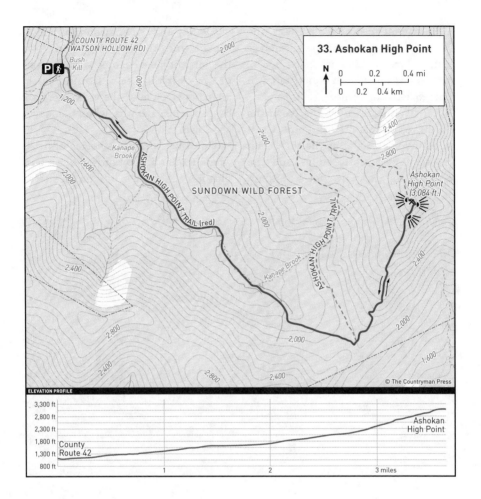

ing the path of the brook. Eventually the ascent begins to steepen, and you will pass stone walls lining the old woods road. At 1.5 miles into the hike, you will hike through mountain laurels before crossing over a second footbridge.

After several stream crossings, the trail veers away from the brook and arrives at a trail junction around the 2.75-mile mark. The trail continuing straight, in a southerly direction, leads to private property and should not be entered. Turn left to leave the woods road and continue up a footpath. Very shortly thereafter, the trail splits once again. Here, the trail to the left will lead up the north loop, a longer route, while the trail to the right will take a shorter, steeper ascent to the summit of the High Point. You can choose to take the south loop trail up and back for a significantly shorter hike, or you can complete a circuit by ascending one trail and descending by another. For this hike, you will be taking the south loop for a there-and-back route. Take the trail to the right, and the path will begin to climb steeply. Ignore unmaintained side trails branching off to the right as you ascend 1,000 feet over the next mile.

After a steep ascent up rocks, the trail will level out, as if the summit is near, before picking up once again. Stone steps have been constructed in spots to help hikers along their way.

At 3.75 miles, you will arrive at the summit of Ashokan High Point. Graffiti dating back as far as the 1800s can still be found scattered around the rocks. To the right are views of Rond-out Valley and the Shawangunk Ridge, though unfortunately the views from the summit have become slightly overgrown over the years. Do not expect an expansive vista—the views here are best in cooler months, when the leaves are down.

Continue through a series of fields where mountaintop homes once stood. Blueberry bushes can be found scattered

THE SERENE SUMMIT OF ASHOKAN HIGH POINT

HAZY LANDSCAPE FROM ATOP ASHOKAN HIGH POINT

around the summit as well. You will come to a camping area with a large fire ring and stone chairs.

From here, you can explore the various side trails around the summit, or, alternatively, continue on the red blazes to follow the longer north loop trail for a longer return down the mountain. The north loop trail is less commonly hiked and more difficult to follow in spots; it is recommended that you simply retrace your steps and return to the parking area following your original route.

34

Vernooy Kill Falls

DISTANCE: 3.4 miles

TYPE: Out and back

TOTAL ELEVATION GAIN: 250'

MAXIMUM ELEVATION: 1,800'

DIFFICULTY: Easy

HIKING TIME: 1 hour

The Vernooy Kill waterfall drops about 30 feet in four sections, with a series of pools making for an ideal summer visit. Indeed, due to the accessibility of the falls, you can expect to find a mix of families and hikers alike enjoying the falls all summer long. The creek and falls were named for Cornelius Vernooy, one of the earliest settlers in the Rondout Valley. About 250 years ago, Vernooy constructed the first gristmill in the region. Partial remains from one of Vernooy's mills still stand near the falls.

GETTING THERE

Take NY-209 to Cherrytown Road, then head north. Cherrytown Road becomes Upper Cherrytown Road. Continue until Upper Cherrytown Road ends at Trails End Road/Sundown Road. Turn left. For the last mile, the road will be a rough, bumpy gravel road with very little space to pass cars coming in the opposite direction. Proceed slowly. The parking area is on the right.

GPS SHORTCUT

Type "Vernooy Kill Falls" into Google Maps and your GPS will navigate you to the appropriate trailhead.

THE TRAIL

Cross the road to the trail and follow the red blazes. The trail leading to the falls is easy to follow and largely level. An old woods road, it is also now designated as a snowmobile trail.

Cross a bridge immediately beyond the trailhead. Shortly after, you will see a clearing to the right of the trail with a makeshift camping area.

After a quarter mile, you will pass

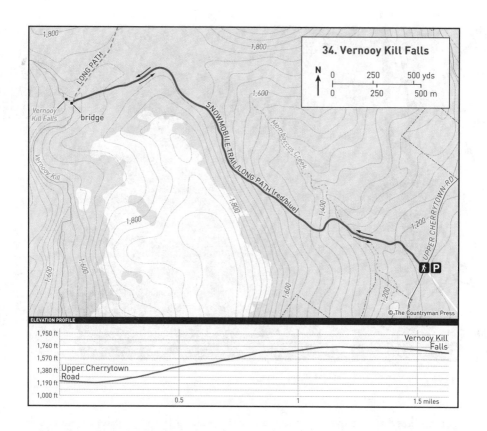

34. Vernooy Kill Falls

N

| 0 | 250 | 500 yds |
| 0 | 250 | 500 m |

ELEVATION PROFILE

Vernooy Kill Falls

Upper Cherrytown Road

1,950 ft
1,760 ft
1,570 ft
1,380 ft
1,190 ft
1,000 ft

0.5   1   1.5 miles

© The Countryman Press

HIKERS ENJOYING A REFRESHING DIP IN THE FALLS

WOODEN TRAIL SIGN POINTING THE WAY TO THE FALLS

a blue-blazed trail to your right. Continue straight on the red-blazed snowmobile trail. The path will remain level and easy.

At an intersection of trails leading to other areas of Sundown Park, you will reach the falls. A wooden bridge crosses the base of the falls, offering an excellent straight-on view. Nearby is a tall stone wall, a remnant of the Vernooy mill. Two centuries ago, this area served as a crossroads where farmers brought their grain for milling.

35

Ashokan Promenade

DISTANCE: 3 miles

TYPE: Out and back

DIFFICULTY: Easy

HIKING TIME: 1 hour

There are few hikes in the Catskills that one might describe as truly easy. Even among those, hikes like Kaaterskill Falls and the Upper Platte Clove Waterfall pose numerous dangers if hikers happen to wander off the trail where they shouldn't. The Ashokan Promenade walk is almost certainly the easiest and safest hike in the whole of the Catskill Park, but no less significant of a destination for that. Indeed, this massive reservoir 13 miles west of the city of Kingston offers an important glimpse into the history of the region and its long, give-and-take relationship with the wealthy metropolis that lies 90 miles to the south.

The Ashokan Reservoir was constructed in the early twentieth century by the New York City Board of Water Supply, and at the time was one of the largest reservoirs in the world. Nonetheless, local opponents to the reservoir argued that, however considerable its size, it still would not be able to hold enough water to meet New York City's needs. After years of negotiations, the reservoir was finally built between 1907 and 1915 by impounding the Esopus Creek and submerging twelve small towns and thousands of acres of farmland. Roughly two thousand residents were displaced by the creation of the reservoir.

The reservoir is the start of the 92-mile-long Catskill Aqueduct, which supplies about 40 percent of New York City's water. At full capacity, the reservoir can hold almost 123 billion US gallons.

GETTING THERE

Take Exit 19 (Kingston) from the New York State Thruway, then make a slight

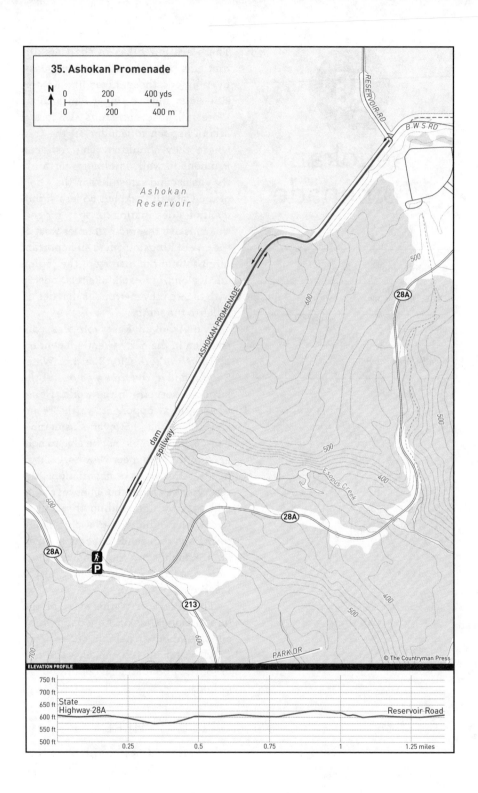

35. Ashokan Promenade

N

| 0 | 200 | 400 yds |
| 0 | 200 | 400 m |

Ashokan
Reservoir

RESERVOIR RD

B W S RD

ASHOKAN PROMENADE

dam
spillway

Esopus Creek

28A

28A

28A

213

PARK DR

© The Countryman Press

ELEVATION PROFILE

750 ft				
700 ft				
650 ft	State			
	Highway 28A		Reservoir Road	
600 ft				
550 ft				
500 ft				
	0.25	0.5	0.75	1	1.25 miles

right onto NY-28 West. Stay on NY-28 West for 3.4 miles, then turn left onto Waughkonk Road. Immediately after, turn right onto NY-28A West. Continue for 10.8 miles. Shortly after you pass the intersection with NY-213, the parking area will be on your right.

GPS SHORTCUT

Typing "Ashokan Promenade Parking Area" into Google Maps will navigate you to the parking area.

THE TRAIL

There aren't many opportunities to get lost at the Ashokan Promenade. While the walkway runs for almost a mile and a half, you will be constrained to the promenade itself for the duration of the walk, an old roadway with guardrails to ensure you don't wander astray.

A barrier has been constructed to prevent cars from the parking area from driving across the promenade. Cross the barrier to find the roadway stretching

HISTORIC SIGHTS NEAR THE WATER'S EDGE

A TRANQUIL VIEW OF ASHOKAN RESERVOIR

straight along the banks of the reservoir. To your left is a sign designating this as the former site of Olive City and Olivebridge, which existed before the construction of the reservoir.

Because this is an active reservoir and thus the water needs to stay clean, activities at Ashokan Reservoir are severely restricted. Boating and logging are by permit only, and it is illegal to bring gas-powered motorboats onto the reservoir, due to concerns of gasoline leakage into the water supply. Swimming is also prohibited. Fortunately, the views over the water (particularly the profile of Ashokan High Point towering to the west) are stunning from just about anywhere.

36

Red Hill Fire Tower

DISTANCE: 2.8 miles	
TYPE: Out and back	
TOTAL ELEVATION GAIN: 850 feet	
MAXIMUM ELEVATION: 2,990 feet	
DIFFICULTY: Easy	
HIKING TIME: 2 hours	

The Red Hill Fire Tower is the southernmost fire tower in the Catskills, as well as one of the last state fire towers built, in 1920, and the last fire tower in the park to have been manned. The Red Hill tower was still staffed through 1990. After this, it was slated to be torn down in accordance with state policy prohibiting nonessential structures on Forest Preserve land. After a campaign by preservationists and forest historians to save the Catskill fire towers, five of the towers (Overlook Mountain, Hunter Mountain, Tremper Mountain, Balsam Lake Mountain, and Red Hill) were restored and added to the National Register of Historic Places. Red Hill's ranger cabin, included as part of the listing, is one of the oldest buildings of its kind in the State of New York.

Red Hill can claim the distinction of being the easiest of the five Catskill fire tower hikes, making it one of the most accessible views of its kind in the park. The trail is a short, relatively undemanding stroll through a quiet, remote section of woods, and the elevation gain you'll face on this hike is relatively tame—for the Catskills, at least. With picnic tables and the stately rangers' cabin offering respite at the midway point, this outing is perfect for a morning or afternoon of quintessential Catskills attractions when you aren't in the mood to sweat too much.

GETTING THERE

Take NY-55 west until it splits with NY-55A, heading northwest along the north side of the Rondout Reservoir. Drive along the length of the reservoir, until 55A reaches Sundown Road. Make a right, then an immediate left onto Sugar-

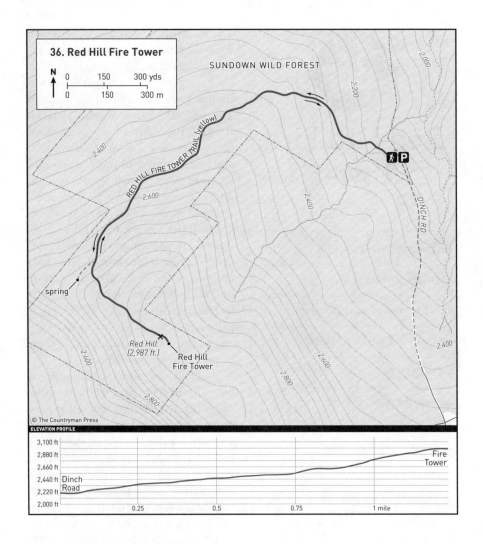

loaf Road. Continue on Sugarloaf Road for 4 miles, then make a sharp left turn onto Dinch Road. Continue on Dinch Road for 1 mile. The parking area will be on the left. The last few hundred feet of the road are not maintained during winter months, so be sure to plan accordingly.

GPS SHORTCUT

Type "Red Hill Fire Tower DEC Parking" into Google Maps and your GPS will navigate you to the appropriate trailhead.

THE TRAIL

The trail begins at the far end of the small parking area. Shortly beyond the trailhead, you will find the trail registration box. Stop and register your hike.

Soon after, you will come to the only stream crossing of the hike. This small stream is seasonal and may not be running during the summer. The trail will begin a moderate ascent as it curves around the mountainside. While rocky in places, the trail is very well maintained and clearly marked.

FOREST LANDSCAPE FROM ATOP RED HILL FIRE TOWER

RANGER CABIN ON THE SUMMIT OF RED HILL

HISTORIC RED HILL FIRE TOWER

Just under a mile into the hike, the incline will pick up, becoming a moderately strenuous uphill hike in places. You will pass a sign indicating a side trail to a water spring.

As you approach the summit, 1.4 miles from the parking area, the trail levels off and the ranger station and its outhouse will come into view. A volunteer staffs the cabin on weekends through the summer, answering questions about the tower and the history of the area, and assisting with visits to the top of the fire tower. From the tower itself, excellent views of the surrounding region can be had on a clear day.

When you are ready to return, retrace your steps back to the parking area.

IV.

CENTRAL

37

Giant Ledge and Panther Mountain

DISTANCE: 6.6 miles

TYPE: Out and back

TOTAL ELEVATION GAIN: 1,555 feet

MAXIMUM ELEVATION: 3,725 feet

DIFFICULTY: Moderate

HIKING TIME: 4.5 hours

With this relatively undemanding hike offering some of the best views in all of the Catskills, it's no surprise that it's also one of the most popular hikes. Giant Ledge gets very busy on weekends, and the parking lot fills up quickly. The succession of easily accessible ledges, each offering a series of spectacular views, are often crowded with enough hikers to create a festive campground atmosphere, a mountain retreat minus the hotel. To have the views to yourself, you may have to visit during a weekday early or late in the season.

Further on, Panther Mountain offers equally stunning views, though similar to those available from Giant Ledge, and only obtained with considerable extra effort. For those looking for a short and easy hike with an immensely rewarding payoff, the first half of this hike can be done on its own—hiking only 1.75 miles to Giant Ledge before turning around and returning to your car. But considering that most of the crowds never make it beyond the ledges, continuing on to Panther Mountain can be worth it for the solitude alone.

GETTING THERE

Take Exit 19 (Kingston) from the New York State Thruway, then turn right onto NY-28. Continue on NY-28 for 30 miles. Turn left onto County Route 47 at Big Indian, then drive for 7.5 miles, heading south. The DEC parking lot will be on your right, immediately before a sharp turn uphill.

GPS SHORTCUT

Type "Panther Mountain trailhead" into Google Maps and your GPS will navigate you to the appropriate trailhead.

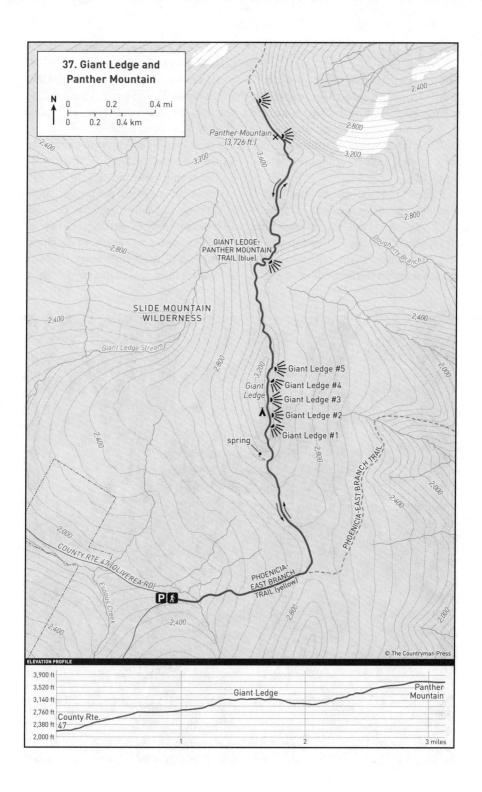

37. Giant Ledge and Panther Mountain

N

| 0 | 0.2 | 0.4 mi |
| 0 | 0.2 | 0.4 km |

Panther Mountain
(3,726 ft.)

GIANT LEDGE-
PANTHER MOUNTAIN
TRAIL (blue)

SLIDE MOUNTAIN
WILDERNESS

Giant Ledge Stream

Giant
Ledge

Giant Ledge #5
Giant Ledge #4
Giant Ledge #3
Giant Ledge #2
Giant Ledge #1

spring

Dougherty Branch

PHOENICIA-EAST BRANCH TRAIL

COUNTY RTE. 47 (OLIVEREA RD)

Esopus Creek

PHOENICIA-
EAST BRANCH
TRAIL (yellow)

2,400
2,800
3,200
3,600
2,000

© The Countryman Press

ELEVATION PROFILE

3,900 ft				
3,520 ft			Giant Ledge	Panther
3,140 ft				Mountain
2,760 ft	County Rte.			
2,380 ft	47			
2,000 ft		1	2	3 miles

THE TRAIL

The trail starts behind a guardrail, uphill from the parking area. Cross the road and go around the guardrail to start on the trail. Register at the DEC registration box, then continue for 0.2 mile before crossing a small footbridge.

Follow the yellow blazes uphill along steep, rocky grade for 0.75 mile until you reach a trail intersection. Here, you will turn left to follow the blue blazes north. You will find a seasonal spring on the left side of the trail, about half a mile after picking up the blue-blazed trail.

After 1.5 miles, you will reach the first ledge, available off a small side trail to the right. Several more ledges will follow shortly, all with incredible views looking out over Woodland Valley toward Slide, Cornell, and Wittenberg.

Between the second and third ledge, there is an area for primitive camping, though no lean-to exists. The trail descends slightly a short distance beyond the campsite before resuming the climb. Just short of the 2-mile mark, you will encounter the fifth and final major ledge.

SIGN MARKING THE TRAIL TO GIANT LEDGE AND PANTHER MOUNTAIN

WINTER LANDSCAPE FROM GIANT LEDGE

From here, if you do not intend to ascend to Panther Mountain, you can turn back to complete the shorter version of this hike. Continuing up the trail toward Panther Mountain, you will soon begin to ascend much more steeply. At milepost 2.75, you will encounter the DEC sign indicating the 3,500-foot elevation mark. Soon after, the trail will begin to level off.

At 3.25 miles in, only a few hundred feet from the summit of the mountain, you will spot a large rock to the right of the trail. Climbing the rock offers views out to the valley below. Continue for another 150 feet past the rock to reach the summit of Panther Mountain.

Continue past the summit for one final viewpoint. This vista also looks out to the Woodland Valley and the mountains beyond, but on a good day, one might even catch a glimpse of the Ashokan Reservoir in the distance.

When you are ready to return, follow the same path back to your car.

Graham Mountain

DISTANCE: 8.3 miles	
TYPE: Out and back	
TOTAL ELEVATION GAIN: 1,285 feet	
MAXIMUM ELEVATION: 3,870 feet	
DIFFICULTY: Moderate	
HIKING TIME: 4 hours	

Graham Mountain has the unique distinction of being the highest privately owned peak in the Catskills. While this is not much of a selling point to hikers, it is made up for by the interesting ruins that can be found on the summit. In the 1960s, a predecessor to the Public Broadcasting Service constructed a relay station on Graham Mountain's peak. The station was abandoned after only a few years, but its remains can still be found there today.

The trail to Graham Mountain splits off from the Dry Brook Ridge Trail, which brings hikers to Balsam Lake Mountain (Guide #39) as well. The two peaks can be done as one hike in a single day, if desired.

GETTING THERE

Take Exit 19 (Kingston) from the New York State Thruway. Turn right onto NY-28, then continue west on NY-28 for about 33 miles. At the Belleayre Ski Center, turn left onto NY-49A. Drive 5 miles until NY-49A ends, then take a left onto Dry Brook Road (NY-49/NY-7A). Drive for 1.4 miles until you come to Mill Brook Road, then take a right. Continue for another 2 miles. The parking area will be on the right side of the road. This is also the parking area for Balsam Lake Mountain and fire tower, which can be done as an extension of this hike.

GPS SHORTCUT

Search Google Maps for "Balsam Lake Mountain, Hardenburgh, NY" and your GPS will navigate you to the appropriate trailhead.

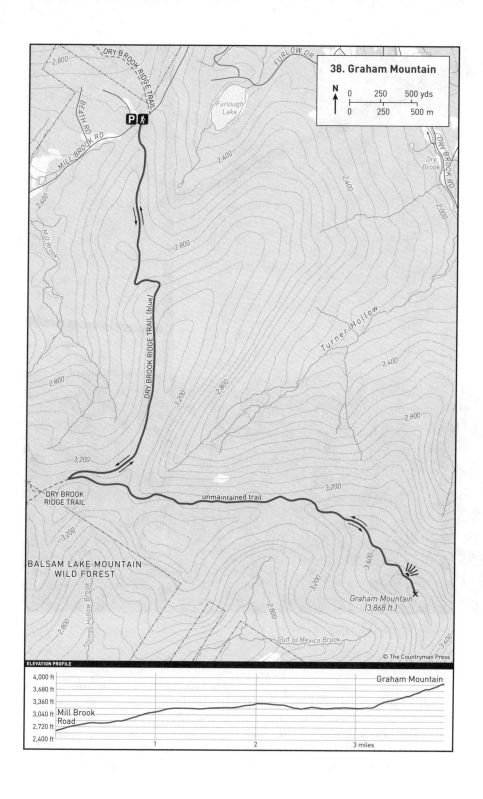

38. Graham Mountain

N

| 0 | 250 | 500 yds |
| 0 | 250 | 500 m |

FURLOW DR

DRY BROOK RIDGE TRAIL

Furlough Lake

2,800

BEATH RD

MILL BROOK RD

P

2,400

2,400

Mill Brook

2,400

Dry Brook

DRY BROOK RD

2,000

2,400

2,400

2,800

2,800

Turner Hollow

2,400

DRY BROOK RIDGE TRAIL (blue)

2,800

3,200

2,800

2,800

3,200

DRY BROOK RIDGE TRAIL

unmaintained trail

3,200

3,200

3,600

BALSAM LAKE MOUNTAIN WILD FOREST

3,200

Youngs Hollow Brook

2,800

2,800

3,200

Graham Mountain (3,868 ft.)

×

3,600

Gulf of Mexico Brook

© The Countryman Press

ELEVATION PROFILE

| 4,000 ft |
| 3,680 ft |
| 3,360 ft |
| 3,040 ft |
| 2,720 ft |
| 2,400 ft |

Graham Mountain

Mill Brook Road

1   2   3 miles

VIEW FROM THE RUINS ON GRAHAM MOUNTAIN

THE TRAIL

From the DEC parking area, walk down the road a short distance to the trailhead. Take the blue-blazed trail heading south—the same Dry Brook Ridge Trail also heads north, toward the Dry Brook Ridge Wild Forest. The beginning of the trail follows an old woods road on private land. You will pass the trail register after a short distance.

Follow the blue blazes as the trail climbs gently. After hiking for a few minutes, you will pass a spring on the right side of the trail. Continue for another mile. Around 2 miles into the hike, you will reach a fork in the trail, with an unmaintained trail heading east toward Graham Mountain. Staying straight on the blue trail would bring you to Balsam Lake Mountain—it is a relatively easy addition, and both peaks are often tackled in the same hike.

Take the trail branching off to the left toward Graham Mountain. Over the next mile, you will climb at a moderate grade toward the summit. The trail is not maintained, and while still easy to follow, it is generally fairly overgrown by late summer.

At the 4-mile mark, you will reach the summit of Graham Mountain. The remains of an old tower can be found in disrepair here. Enjoy the views—Balsam Lake Mountain and the fire tower on its peak can be seen nearby. Looking southeast you can see Doubletop Mountain, the tallest peak in the Catskills without an established trail leading to the summit.

When you are ready to return, retrace your steps to your car.

VIEW OF GRAHAM MOUNTAIN FROM NEARBY BALSAM LAKE MOUNTAIN

Balsam Lake Mountain and Fire Tower

DISTANCE: 7.5 miles	
TYPE: Lollipop	
TOTAL ELEVATION GAIN: 1,150 feet	
MAXIMUM ELEVATION: 3,730 feet	
DIFFICULTY: Moderate	
HIKING TIME: 4 hours	

Located at the southern tip of the Dry Brook Ridge, this pleasant circuit hike features relatively easy trail grade along an old woods road, and it rewards hikers with views from a very nice fire tower on the summit. A large grassy clearing surrounds the fire tower and makes a great place to picnic. This is an enjoyable hike any time of year, and it can be easily snowshoed in winter months. Be sure to stay on the footpath, as the first few miles of the trail cross private property.

GETTING THERE

Take Exit 19 (Kingston) from the New York State Thruway. Turn right onto NY-28 West, then continue west on NY-28 for about 33 miles. At the Belleayre Ski Center, turn left onto NY-49A. Drive 5 miles, until NY-49A ends, then take a left onto Dry Brook Road (NY-49/NY-7A). Drive for 1.4 miles until you come to Mill Brook Road, then take a right onto Mill Brook Road. Continue for another 2 miles. The parking area will be on the right side of the road. This is also the parking area for Graham Mountain (Guide #38), which can be done as an extension of this hike.

GPS SHORTCUT

Type "Balsam Lake Mountain" into Google Maps and your GPS will navigate you to the appropriate trailhead.

THE TRAIL

From the DEC parking area, walk down the road a short distance to the trailhead. Take the blue-blazed trail heading south—the same Dry Brook Ridge Trail also heads north, toward the Dry Brook

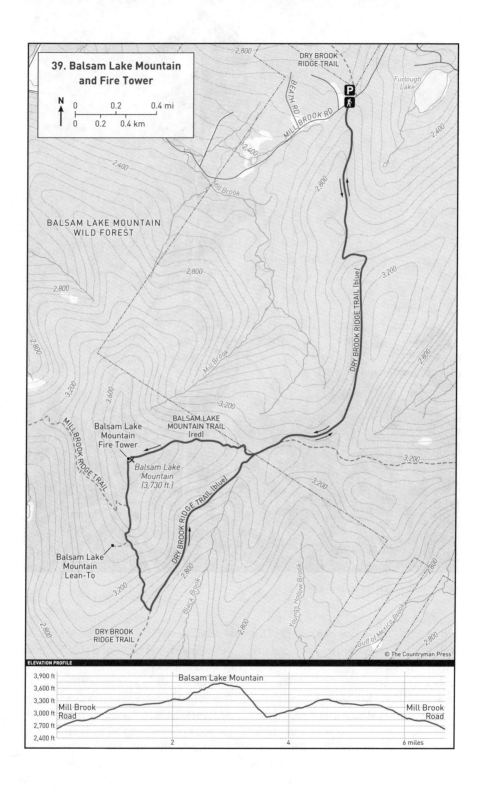

39. Balsam Lake Mountain and Fire Tower

N

0   0.2   0.4 mi
0   0.2   0.4 km

DRY BROOK RIDGE TRAIL

Furlough Lake

BEATH RD

MILL BROOK RD

2,800

2,400

2,800

2,400

BALSAM LAKE MOUNTAIN WILD FOREST

2,400

Mill Brook

2,800

2,800

2,800

3,200

3,200

DRY BROOK RIDGE TRAIL (blue)

Mill Brook

3,200

BALSAM LAKE MOUNTAIN TRAIL (red)

Balsam Lake Mountain Fire Tower

Balsam Lake Mountain (3,730 ft.)

MILLBROOK RIDGE TRAIL

3,200

3,600

3,200

DRY BROOK RIDGE TRAIL (blue)

Balsam Lake Mountain Lean-To

3,200

2,800

Black Brook

2,800

Youngs Hollow Brook

Gulf of Mexico Brook

2,800

2,800

DRY BROOK RIDGE TRAIL

© The Countryman Press

ELEVATION PROFILE

3,900 ft	Balsam Lake Mountain	
3,600 ft		
3,300 ft		
3,000 ft	Mill Brook Road	Mill Brook Road
2,700 ft		
2,400 ft	2 4 6 miles	

BALSAM LAKE MOUNTAIN FIRE TOWER

Ridge Wild Forest. The beginning of the trail follows an old woods road on private land. You will pass the trail register after a short distance.

Follow the blue blazes as the trail climbs gently. After hiking for a few minutes, you will pass a spring on the right side of the trail. Continue for another mile. Around 2 miles into the hike, you will pass a trail on your left,

headed east. This is an unmaintained but easily discernible trail that leads to Graham Mountain.

Shortly after you pass the trail to Graham Mountain, you will arrive at an official trail junction, with a red-blazed trail leading to the right. Take this trail. The blue-blazed Dry Brook Ridge Trail continues straight toward Balsam Lake. You will return on this trail, following the loop around Balsam Lake Mountain.

Follow the red blazes as the trail becomes steeper. Continue for another 0.75 mile, until the tower comes into view. You will pass the ranger station just before reaching the summit. As with all Catskill fire towers (the others can be found on Hunter Mountain, Overlook Mountain, Red Hill, and Tremper Mountain), the ranger station is staffed seasonally on weekends, with volunteers present to answer questions and help you safely ascend the tower.

Rising above the treetops, the restored tower offers excellent views in all directions. Views of the Pepacton Reservoir, Dry Brook Valley, Belleayre, Balsam Mountain , Big Indian, Bearpen Mountain, and more can be had on a good day.

The trail continues downhill past an outhouse. After about a quarter of a mile, you will continue straight through an intersection with the yellow-blazed Millbrook Ridge Trail, which heads west toward Alder Lake. A short distance later you will pass a side trail leading off to the right for the Balsam Lake Mountain Lean-To. There is also a water source near the shelter. Continue south until you reconnect with the blue-blazed Dry Brook Ridge Trail. Turn left and follow the blue blazes back to the parking area.

IN THE OBSERVATION TOWER ON BALSAM LAKE MOUNTAIN

40
Alder Lake Loop

DISTANCE: 2 miles

TYPE: Loop

TOTAL ELEVATION GAIN: 75 feet

MAXIMUM ELEVATION: 2250 feet

DIFFICULTY: Easy

HIKING TIME: 1 hour

A popular spot for swimmers and families, Alder Lake is a man-made lake created in 1901 by Samuel D. Coykendall, a prominent figure in the area with ties to regional railroads. In addition to the lake, Coykendall constructed the Coykendall Lodge, a three-story home built as a summer escape for his family. After Coykendall's death, the lodge changed owners several times before the state acquired the property in 1980. After a long period of neglect and decay, the building was eventually demolished in 2008. The stone foundation can still be found near the beginning of the hike today.

GETTING THERE

From NY-17 heading north, take Exit 96 at Livingston Manor, then turn right onto Debruce Road. After half a mile, turn right onto Old Route 17/Rock Avenue, and drive for 1.3 miles. Make a slight right onto Beaverkill Road and drive for 11 miles. Make another slight right to stay on Beaverkill Road and continue another 1.4 miles. Turn left onto Alder Road. After 2 miles, turn right onto Cross Mountain Road to reach the parking area.

GPS SHORTCUT

Type "Alder Lake, Hardenburgh, NY" into Google Maps to have your GPS navigate you to the appropriate trailhead.

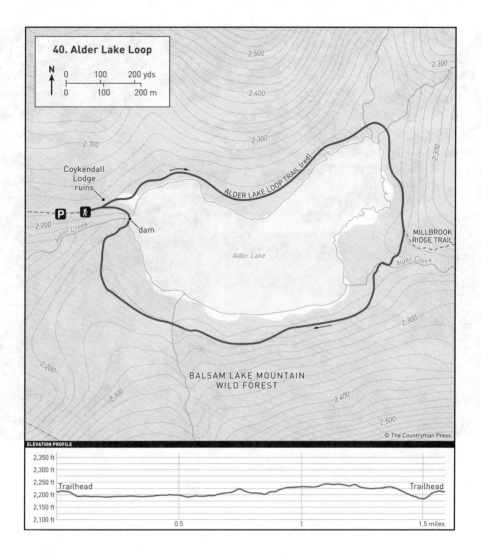

THE TRAIL

From the parking area, locate the trail past the foundation of the Coykendall Lodge. Walk down the right side of the ruins to follow the trail around the lake. The loop around Alder Lake is one of the easiest in the Catskills, with no significant elevation change. Along the way, you will pass a number of campsites and access points to the lake. Fishing is allowed here seasonally.

On the other side of the lake, you will reach Cradle Rock Ridge. After 0.8 mile the Millbrook Ridge Trail (yellow blazes) turns left. Stay straight on the main trail to continue around the lake. Soon, cross a bridge over Alder Creek.

Continue on the woods road. Close to the southern end of the lake, you will arrive at an open area. Cross the dam and walk up the path to return to your car.

EARLY MORNING MIST ON ALDER LAKE

Kelly Hollow Loop

DISTANCE: 3.7 miles

TYPE: Loop

TOTAL ELEVATION GAIN: 500 feet

MAXIMUM ELEVATION: 2,250 feet

DIFFICULTY: Easy

HIKING TIME: 3 hours

Located in the Balsam Lake Mountain Wild Forest, the Kelly Hollow loop offers hikers a scenic, relatively quiet walk through varied forest on well-graded ski trails. As a result, the route can be hiked any time of year without much difficulty and can be cross-country skied in the winter. Much of the trail edges unnamed streams that feed Mill Brook, giving hikers occasional glimpses of small nearby waterfalls. A connector trail about halfway through the circuit allows for an option to shorten the hike, making this a great outing for families or anyone looking for a more relaxed day. On the other hand, a shelter near the southern tip of the trail and a couple of nice campsites give hikers the option of turning a day hike into a short, easy overnight trip. Because of this, the Kelly Hollow loop would be a great introduction to backpacking for interested but inexperienced parties. Although this trail lacks any vistas or viewpoints, the real draw of this hike lies in the solitude and options to shorten or lengthen the hike to your liking.

GETTING THERE

Take Exit 19 (Kingston) from the New York State Thruway. Turn right onto NY-28 West, then continue west on NY-28 for about 42 miles, until you reach the hamlet of Arkville. Just after passing through Arkville, turn onto Dry Brook Road. Follow Dry Brook Road for 6.3 miles and turn right onto Mill Brook Road. Drive 5.8 miles and pass the Grants Mills covered bridge on the right. There are two DEC parking areas a mile up the road on the left. The hike starts at the second parking area.

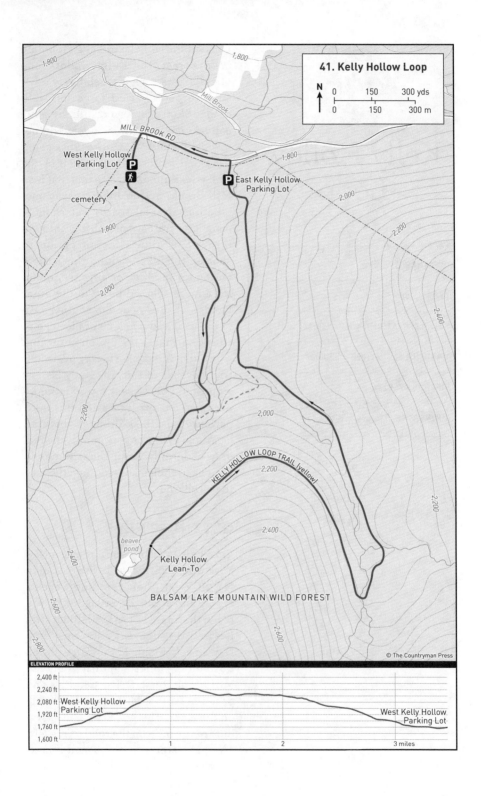

41. Kelly Hollow Loop

N

| 0 | 150 | 300 yds |
| 0 | 150 | 300 m |

1,800

Mill Brook

MILL BROOK RD

1,800

West Kelly Hollow
Parking Lot

cemetery

East Kelly Hollow
Parking Lot

1,800

1,800

2,000

2,000

2,200

2,400

2,200

2,000

1,800

2,000

KELLY HOLLOW LOOP TRAIL (yellow)

2,200

2,200

2,200

2,400

beaver
pond

Kelly Hollow
Lean-To

BALSAM LAKE MOUNTAIN WILD FOREST

2,400

2,600

2,600

2,800

© The Countryman Press

ELEVATION PROFILE

| 2,400 ft |
| 2,240 ft |
| 2,080 ft | West Kelly Hollow |
| 1,920 ft | Parking Lot |
| 1,760 ft |
| 1,600 ft |

West Kelly Hollow
Parking Lot

1   2   3 miles

ENTERING THE GRAND PINE STAND IN KELLY HOLLOW

GPS SHORTCUT

Type "Grants Mills Covered Bridge" into Google Maps. The trailhead is a mile west on Mill Brook Road.

THE TRAIL

The trailhead starts at the end of the parking area, near an old cemetery and two grassy campsites. There are eroding gravestones in the cemetery dating back to the early nineteenth century, and the site is well worth taking a stroll through if you have the time.

From the dirt road, walk south into the woods and pick up a yellow-blazed ski trail. Begin gradually climbing on old, rocky roadbed, eventually skirting the edge of a steep drop to your left. There is an unnamed run in the ravine below. As you walk, keep an eye out for glimpses of small waterfalls along this stream.

Continue climbing through hemlock groves for 0.8 mile until you reach the connector trail on your left, marked by a sign. From here you have two options. Turning left will bisect the circuit, leading you to the other side of the stream in 0.2 mile. This option will shorten the loop by 2 miles. Turning right will send you up a steeper trail for another 0.2 mile before leveling off significantly.

Turn right and continue to climb until you reach a grassy clearing, where you'll find a picturesque view of a beaver pond. The trail circles the pond, giving you plenty of time to enjoy the area. In 0.5 mile from the connector trail split, reach a well-used lean-to near the edge of the beaver pond. This is a good place to take a break and further explore the pond, as there is easy access to the water's edge nearby.

Continue hiking on fairly level terrain for roughly 0.7 mile, at which point the trail turns sharply to your left. Cross a small seasonal run and enter a majestic pine stand, eventually crossing another run in about 500 feet. This section of trail is fairly level, giving you the opportunity to take in your surroundings as you walk beside another unnamed stream that will eventually feed into the first. The trail descends moderately for another 0.6 mile before you reach the connector trail on your left. Follow the main trail for another 0.5 mile, descending on rocky road grade until you reach the second parking area. Just before the parking area, there is a large campsite along the stream on the left, 100 feet into the woods.

Walk to the road from this parking area and turn left. You will roadwalk the final 0.3 mile to reach your vehicle at the other parking area.

BEAVER POND NEAR THE KELLY HOLLOW SHELTER

42

Pakatakan Mountain

DISTANCE: 3.4 miles

TYPE: Out and back

TOTAL ELEVATION GAIN: 1,030 feet

MAXIMUM ELEVATION: 2,430 feet

DIFFICULTY: Difficult

HIKING TIME: 3 hours

Located just outside the town of Margaretville, the hike to Pakatakan Mountain is a short jaunt up the northern tip of the Dry Brook Ridge. Don't let the length fool you, though! You will have to work to gain the ridge, as the trail climbs more than 1,000 feet in just under 2 miles. The trail has a tendency to zigzag back and forth, leveling off in places just long enough for you to catch your breath before sending you scrambling uphill again.

Beyond Pakatakan Mountain the trail continues, passing through Dry Brook Ridge Wild Forest and Balsam Lake Mountain Wild Forest, traversing the entire length of the ridge, before ending at the southern base of Balsam Lake Mountain almost 14 miles from the northern terminus. The portion of the trail this hike follows is usually quiet, and it ascends by means of a well-graded jeep road, so you'll have plenty of opportunities to take in the forest scenery as you're making the trek uphill.

GETTING THERE

Take Exit 19 (Kingston) from the New York State Thruway. Turn right onto NY-28 West, then continue west on NY-28 for approximately 42 miles, until you reach the village of Margaretville. You will go straight through a light at the junction of Bridge Street, which crosses the East Branch Delaware River and heads into Margaretville. A little less than half a mile after passing Bridge Street, turn left onto Fair Street. Follow Fair Street for 0.3 mile, and make a sharp left onto Southside Road. The parking area is on the left side of the road about a quarter of a mile from where Fair Street ends, on the wide grassy shoulder. There should be a trail

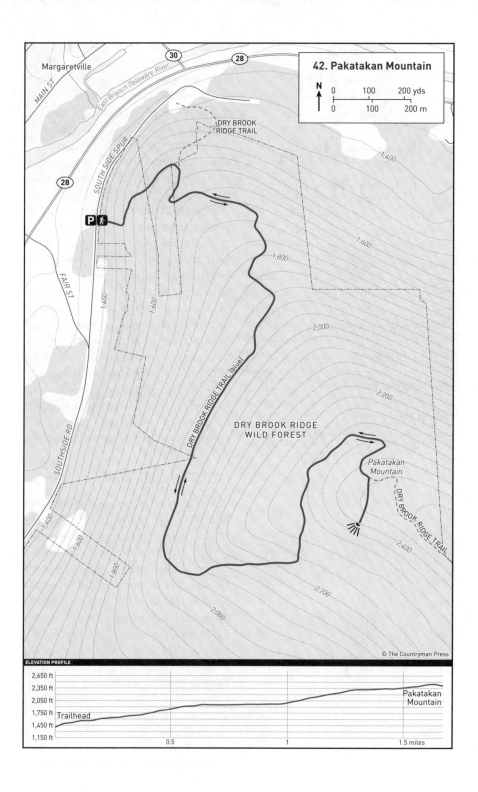

42. Pakatakan Mountain

N 0 100 200 yds
0 100 200 m

Margaretville

MAIN ST
30
28
East Branch Delaware River
SOUTH SIDE SPUR
28
FAIR ST
SOUTHSIDE RD

DRY BROOK
RIDGE TRAIL

1,400
1,600
1,800
2,000
2,200
2,400

DRY BROOK RIDGE TRAIL (blue)

DRY BROOK RIDGE
WILD FOREST

Pakatakan
Mountain

DRY BROOK RIDGE TRAIL

© The Countryman Press

ELEVATION PROFILE

2,650 ft			
2,350 ft			Pakatakan
2,050 ft			Mountain
1,750 ft	Trailhead		
1,450 ft			
1,150 ft	0.5	1	1.5 miles

register on the edge of the woods opposite the parking area.

GPS SHORTCUT

Inputting "Pakatakan Mountain" into Google Maps will not bring you to the appropriate trailhead. To reach the start of the trail, you may type "S Side Spur, Margaretville, NY" into Google Maps and your GPS will navigate you very close to the trailhead.

THE TRAIL

From the parking area, cross the road and sign in to the aforementioned DEC trail register. Head into the woods on the Dry Brook Ridge Trail, which is marked with blue blazes. The trail ascends quickly for a few hundred feet as soon as you enter the woods. Turn left onto an old logging road and continue climbing more moderately than before, passing several interesting stone ledges with large cave-like overhangs. The trail levels off for a short distance and then bends back to the right, resuming the climb as you cross over the Dry Brook Ridge Wild Forest boundary.

Continue to follow the blue blazes through an old hemlock grove; the trail opens eventually into mixed forest dominated by maples and oaks. There are more ledgy overhangs as the trail progresses, turning back and forth on large, lazy switchbacks. After about half a mile of moderate to steep climbing, the trail will begin to turn to the right and level off. Catch your breath as you walk this easy grade for another half mile, continuing to follow the blue blazes. If you are hiking in the summer or early fall, you might be able to smell

A ROCK FORMATION ON THE WAY TO THE SUMMIT OF PAKATAKAN MOUNTAIN

VIEW FROM THE SUMMIT OF PAKATAKAN MOUNTAIN

the fern patches that grow alongside the forest road.

Approximately a mile from the trailhead, you will come to a split in the road. To the right is a seasonal spring, marked with a wooden sign. The spring is located roughly 100 feet from the fork in the trail, although it may not be running during dry periods. The main trail turns to the left and resumes a fairly aggressive climb, with beech trees becoming more common as you ascend.

After climbing for 0.25 mile, the grade will begin to lessen as the trail turns to the left. As you walk, you will notice even more rock formations slightly off-trail to the right. In a short distance, the trail curves back to the right, ascending once again as you circumnavigate a craggy ledge near the top of the mountain.

Shortly after passing over the ledge, the trail becomes much more level, and a herd path breaks off of the main trail to the right. The path may be hard to distinguish if snow or leaves are covering the trail, so be alert. It is located just after a tree bearing a blue trail marker. Follow the herd path, and in a few hundred feet you will reach a grassy clearing on a stone outcropping. This is the viewpoint on Pakatakan Mountain, 1.7 miles from the trailhead. From here you can see partially obstructed views of the surrounding hills and valleys, as well as Pepacton Reservoir and the East Branch Delaware River to the west.

From the viewing area, you will notice a second herd path heading back into the woods toward the Dry Brook Ridge Trail. Follow this herd path until you come to the main trail. Turn left here and follow the blue blazes back downhill to the parking area.

43

Belleayre Mountain Ridge

DISTANCE: 6.3 miles

TYPE: Out and back

TOTAL ELEVATION GAIN: 2,260 feet

MAXIMUM ELEVATION: 2,550 feet

DIFFICULTY: Strenuous

HIKING TIME: 3.5 hours

Belleayre Mountain is a popular ski resort, and the sight of the empty, abandoned-seeming mountain lodge and ski lifts in the off-season adds a layer of intrigue to this otherwise simple but strenuous hike. The views from the skiing areas are excellent, though this route remains under the radar compared to others in the region, and on the right day, you will likely find yourself alone among the empty resort structures, feeling as if you've stumbled upon postapocalyptic ruins.

Another unusual feature of this trail is how challenging the ascent is, on an otherwise arrow-straight and unremarkable-seeming woods road trail. Shooting straight up the mountain without a switchback in sight, the trail will immediately begin its climb of 1,300 feet over the next 1.3 miles. The broad, road-like trail helps buffer somewhat against the challenge of this climb, but expect to be winded and sweaty before taking in the sights at the top.

This trail is an easement on private land, so be sure to stay on the trail at all times.

GETTING THERE

Take Exit 19 (Kingston) from the New York State Thruway. Turn right onto NY-28 West, then continue west on NY-28 for about 27 miles. At Big Indian, turn onto Route 47 heading southwest. Continue for half a mile, then take a right onto Lost Clove Road. Continue for 1.5 miles until you see the designated parking area on the right. The road dead-ends just after this.

GPS SHORTCUT

Search Google Maps for "Lost Clove Road, Big Indian, NY." Follow the road

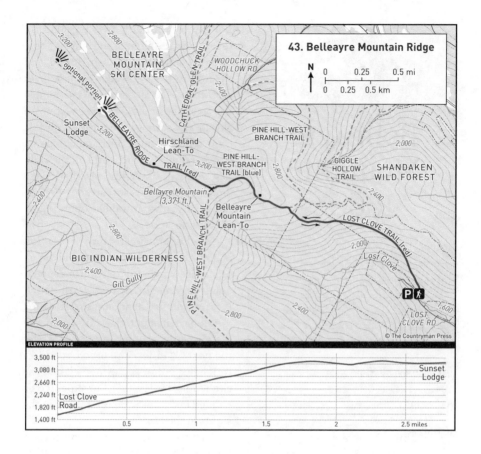

© The Countryman Press

all the way to the end to reach the trailhead.

THE TRAIL

Walk straight ahead from the parking area onto the red-blazed trail. You will begin the steep ascent almost immediately. Very similar to the hike up Overlook Mountain (Guide #18), the trail here is fairly unremarkable, very easy to follow, and unrelenting. It is a tedious and grueling ascent, but the sights at the top of Belleayre are worth it. As there are no obvious break points during the climb, hike at whatever pace you feel comfortable, take breaks when you need, and remind yourself again

and again that at least this is much better exercise than taking the ski lift up.

After 1.3 miles, the Lost Clove Trail enters the Forest Preserve, and shortly after that, it meets the blue-blazed Pine Hill–West Branch Trail, where the red trail ends.

Turn left onto the blue trail and continue toward the summit of Belleayre Mountain. The ascent gets somewhat easier here, and after about a quarter of a mile, you will see a lean-to on the right through the trees. Continue past the lean-to for another half mile to the summit of Belleayre Mountain. Due to tree cover, the summit does not offer any views, but you will see the founda-

VIEW FROM ATOP BELLEAYRE RIDGE

tion of an old fire tower that stood until the 1980s.

The Pine Hill–West Branch trail will now turn south toward Balsam Mountain. Instead, walk through the field that covers the summit. Slightly to your right, pick up the red-blazed Belleayre Ridge Trail.

You will see a second lean-to just off the trail after about 0.3 miles. Continue straight. The trail widens, and remains fairly level, though the trail is less clearly marked here. You will begin to see signs for the various ski slopes before finally arriving at the lifts and the resort's Sunset Lodge. The lodge, empty and locked up during the off-season, still offers a pleasant place to sit and rest. Balsam Mountain is visible in the distance to the south.

If the sights of the slopes and structures around the Sunset Lodge aren't enough for you, you can continue walking straight ahead on the path all the way out to Deer Run, the last lift and ski slope on the ridge. When you are ready, return along the same route to your vehicle. The trail will seem astonishingly short now that you're going downhill!

SKI LIFT ON BELLEAYRE MOUNTAIN

44

Balsam Mountain

DISTANCE: 5.2 miles

TYPE: Loop

TOTAL ELEVATION GAIN: 1,600 feet

MAXIMUM ELEVATION: 3,600 feet

DIFFICULTY: Moderate

HIKING TIME: 3 hours

Not to be confused with Balsam Lake Mountain, which is located to the southwest, Balsam Mountain sits south of the Belleayre Ridge, and can be climbed a number of different ways. The hike described here follows the shortest route, a pleasant loop starting from the west side of the mountain. The peak can be hiked from the east as well, but that route is a mile longer and climbs an additional 400 feet on very steep trail. Balsam is a popular destination for hikers, as it is a required climb for peak baggers seeking membership in the Catskill 3500 Club. Members of the club must climb all thirty-five Catskill peaks over 3,500 feet in elevation, and must also climb four designated peaks for a second time in the winter. Balsam is one of those mountains, along with Panther, Slide, and Blackhead.

GETTING THERE

Take Exit 19 (Kingston) from the New York State Thruway. Turn right onto NY-28 West, then continue west on NY-28 for approximately 36 miles. About a mile after passing through the village of Pine Hill, turn left onto Galli Curci Road, and pass the Belleayre Ski Center shortly thereafter. Follow Galli Curci Road as it winds over the shoulder of the mountain, and merge onto Todd Mountain Road as you descend. In roughly 2 miles, turn left onto Rider Hollow Road and follow it. The parking area is at the end of Rider Hollow Road, 2 miles from the junction with Todd Mountain Road.

GPS SHORTCUT

Type "Rider Hollow, Hardenburgh, NY" into Google Maps to have your GPS navigate you very close to the appropriate

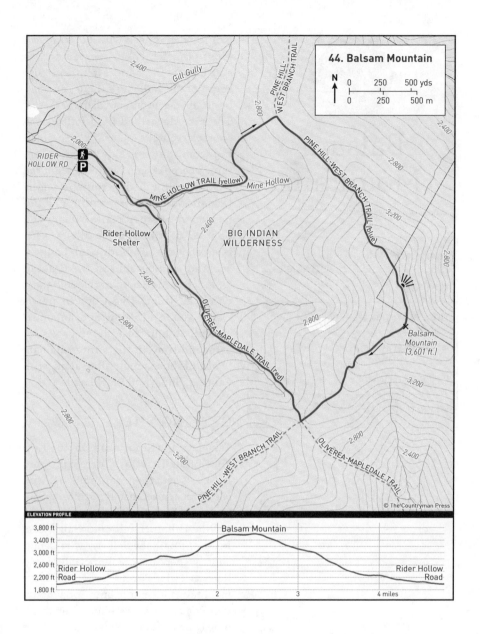

N
0   250   500 yds
0   250   500 m

Gill Gully
2,400

PINE HILL–
WEST BRANCH TRAIL

2,800

2,400

PINE HILL–WEST BRANCH TRAIL (blue)

2,800

RIDER
HOLLOW RD

2,000

MINE HOLLOW TRAIL (yellow)   Mine Hollow

3,200

2,800

Rider Hollow
Shelter

2,400

BIG INDIAN
WILDERNESS

2,400

OLIVEREA–MAPLEDALE TRAIL (red)

2,800

2,800

Balsam
Mountain
(3,601 ft.)

2,800

3,200

3,200

PINE HILL–WEST BRANCH TRAIL

OLIVEREA–MAPLEDALE TRAIL

2,800

2,400

3,200

© The Countryman Press

ELEVATION PROFILE

		Balsam Mountain		
3,800 ft				
3,400 ft				
3,000 ft				
2,600 ft	Rider Hollow			Rider Hollow
2,200 ft	Road			Road
1,800 ft				

1   2   3   4 miles

trailhead. From there, follow the instructions above to reach the parking area.

THE TRAIL

From the parking area, pass a gate and
head into the forest on a wide forest road.
Remember to sign in at the DEC register.
You will start hiking on the red-blazed

Oliverea-Mapledale Trail, passing a herd
path to your right immediately after
entering the woods. The herd path will
take you to a small, underused campsite
roughly a hundred feet off-trail. There
are a handful of other primitive campsites that you will pass on this hike, farther up the trail, as well as a shelter. The
campsites and shelter are available on

MARKERS ON MOST TRAILS DESIGNATE THE 3,500 FOOT ELEVATION LINE

a first-come-first-served basis, and they would be perfect for transforming this relaxed day hike into a full-blown weekend expedition.

Hike up the red-blazed trail, and reach a footbridge crossing over a stream in a few hundred feet. Once on the other side, pass the remnants of an old stone fence and continue walking along the stream. In a short distance the trail will veer to the left, leaving the road grade that follows the stream and sending you uphill, climbing moderately. In 0.3 miles you will come to a trail junction. The Oliverea-Mapledale Trail continues to the right, and the yellow-blazed Mine Hollow Trail starts to the left. Turn left and begin walking on the Mine Hollow Trail. This is the start of the loop portion of the hike. You will ascend on a slightly rockier grade, level off for a short distance, and descend to a seasonal streambed. There is a nice open campsite under some old hemlock trees to your right here. Turn left, following the yellow blazes uphill along the streambed. When you reach a grove of large hemlock trees, the trail will cut to the left sharply and climb more aggressively than before. This steep section is fairly brief. When you reach the base of a large stone ledge, turn right and follow the trail as it weaves around the back side, sending you over another smaller ledge shortly. The trail will level off significantly as you gain the ridge of the mountain range and come to the intersection of the Pine Hill–West Branch Trail. The Mine Hollow Trail ends here, a mile from where it splits from the red-blazed trail.

Turn right and follow the blue blazes of the Pine Hill–West Branch Trail as it undulates along the ridgeline. The trail passes sections of forest overgrown with small beech and birch saplings before opening up in an area that is home to several very large maple and oak trees. The trail becomes steeper on the other side of this open area, climbing a short distance up a rocky section. From the top of this cliff you might be able see Belleayre Mountain through the trees looking north, as long as the canopy isn't too thick.

The incline of the trail mellows a little further on, although you will still climb moderately. Continue to follow the trail, and after a short distance you will come to a sign alerting you that you've reached 3,500 feet above sea level. From here you will start to see balsam firs more prominently. The trail levels after this point, following the lip of the ridge, taking you

BRIDGED STREAM CROSSING ON THE BALSAM MOUNTAIN LOOP

DEVIL'S PATH ON THE SKYLINE NEAR THE SUMMIT OF BALSAM MOUNTAIN

to a grassy clearing, which will be on your left. Although you are not at the summit yet, this is an excellent place to stop and enjoy a snack. You can see the town of Big Indian in the valley below, nestled at the foot of the long sloping ridge closest to you, which leads to the summit of Panther Mountain. Further back, looking left to right, you can see Sherrill Mountain and North Dome, as well as the Devil's Path range fading into the distance.

When you are ready to resume your hike, continue up the blue-blazed path climbing a short distance to the top of Balsam Mountain. At this point you have travelled 1.3 miles on the Pine Hill–West Branch Trail. There are no views from here, and you will begin descending on the same trail immediately after crossing the summit. The descent is about as steep as the climb up, but the trail is much rockier on this side of the mountain.

In 0.8 mile from the summit, the red-blazed Oliverea-Mapledale Trail intersects with the Pine Hill–West Branch Trail at the col between Balsam Mountain and Haynes Mountain. Turn right here, and follow the red blazes downhill. You will be thankful that you are descending on this trail, as it is much steeper than your climb up was. Cross over seasonal creek beds a few times as you make your way downhill, and come to the junction of the Mine Hollow Trail in 1.45 miles. A tenth of a mile before reaching the trail junction, you will pass Rider Hollow Shelter. There are two nice primitive campsites nearby, a little further up the trail, just before it crosses a stream over an old metal bridge.

Pass the junction of the Mine Hollow Trail and continue to follow the red blazes, descending to the water's edge. Cross the footbridge near the trailhead and reach the parking area shortly thereafter.

45

Burroughs Memorial/ Rochester Hollow

DISTANCE: 6.1 miles	
TYPE: Lollipop	
TOTAL ELEVATION GAIN: 840 feet	
MAXIMUM ELEVATION: 2,290 feet	
DIFFICULTY: Moderate	
HIKING TIME: 3 hours	

Nestled in the quiet Shandaken Wild Forest, the Rochester Hollow Loop is truly a hidden gem, giving hikers a glimpse of what life in the Catskill Mountains must have been like long ago. You will walk on well-blazed trails beside the foundations of old farmhouses and the stone fences that accompanied them. The forest is varied, transitioning from mostly hemlock to birches, maples, and oaks about halfway through your climb. The trail system here is a designated mountain bike path and is very well graded. For this reason, Rochester Hollow is a treat to visit any time of year and can be travelled by ski, snowshoe, bike, or foot.

GETTING THERE

Take Exit 19 (Kingston) from the New York State Thruway. Turn right onto NY-28 West, then continue west on NY-28 for about 28 miles, through the hamlet of Big Indian, before turning right onto Matyas Road. The parking area is in front of a gate at the end of Matyas Road.

GPS SHORTCUT

Type "Rochester Hollow" into Google Maps and your GPS will navigate you to the appropriate trailhead.

THE TRAIL

From the parking area, pass behind the gate and start hiking north on the blue-blazed Colonel Rochester Trail. Be sure to sign in at the DCNR trail register a few hundred feet up the trail from the parking area. Much of this trail is on an old woods road that parallels a quaint stream just to your left, occasionally

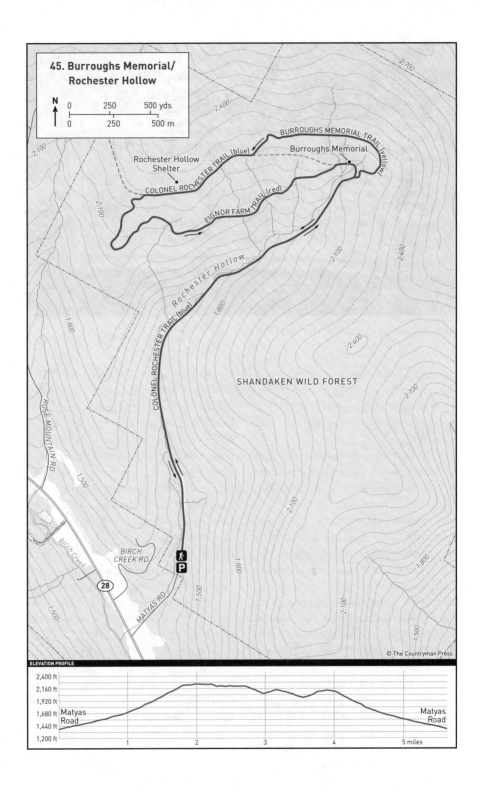

45. Burroughs Memorial/ Rochester Hollow

N

| 0 | 250 | 500 yds |
| 0 | 250 | 500 m |

BURROUGHS MEMORIAL TRAIL (yellow)

COLONEL ROCHESTER TRAIL (blue)

Rochester Hollow Shelter

Burroughs Memorial

COLONEL ROCHESTER TRAIL (blue)

EIGNOR FARM TRAIL (red)

Rochester Hollow

COLONEL ROCHESTER TRAIL (blue)

SHANDAKEN WILD FOREST

ROSE MOUNTAIN RD

Birch Creek

BIRCH CREEK RD

28

MATYAS RD

© The Countryman Press

ELEVATION PROFILE

2,400 ft	
2,160 ft	
1,920 ft	
1,680 ft	Matyas Road ... Matyas Road
1,440 ft	
1,200 ft	

1 2 3 4 5 miles

MEMORIAL DEDICATED TO NATURE AUTHOR JOHN BURROUGHS

punctuated with small, babbling rapids. The climb is relatively gradual and the trail is easy, so you'll have plenty of opportunity to enjoy the forest as you walk.

Very shortly after leaving the parking area, you will pass a large campsite on your left, and another in about 0.25 mile. These campsites would be nice for a relaxed overnight trip, given their proximity to the parking area and the ease of access to plenty of water.

Continue climbing, eventually reaching the remains of a stone gate approximately 1.1 miles from the parking area. The trail will gradually begin to level off as you proceed, and in another 0.65 mile, the yellow-blazed Burroughs Memorial Trail comes in from the right. The Colonel Rochester Trail continues on, meeting back up with the Burroughs Memorial Trail in 0.4 mile. Following the blue blazes gives you the option to shorten the hike slightly, knocking 0.4 mile off your total mileage.

Turn right and follow the yellow-blazed Burroughs Memorial Trail. This trail leaves the woods road behind, winding uphill through impressive maple and beech stands, gaining another 170 feet of elevation to bring you to the high point of this hike. As you walk, pass a plethora of old stone fences and a few foundations. There are perhaps half a dozen of these fences, running for hundreds of feet, dividing the forest on either side of the trail. This is definitely one of the highlights of this hike, so be sure to explore and enjoy these antiquated structures. Let your mind wander, imagining what it must have been like to live in these woods so long ago, before moving on.

In 0.8 mile the Burroughs Memorial Trail ends, dropping you back onto the woods road and the Colonel Rochester Trail. Turn right and resume following the blue blazes, passing through the ruins of the Rochester Estate in 0.3 mile. Further up the trail a short distance lies the very well-maintained Rochester Hollow Shelter, giving backpackers yet another option for a short overnight stay. The lean-to will be slightly uphill on the right. This shelter is a good place to rest and enjoy the serene silence of the surrounding forest.

Leave the shelter, following the woods road west for 0.1 mile, and meet the red-blazed Eignor Farm Trail on the left. Follow this trail downhill, shortly passing by a huge maple tree that sits on the perimeter of a small grassy clearing. Continue on for 1.35 miles through towering oaks on occasionally rocky terrain. As the trail begins to climb again, you will weave your way through more stone walls, running downhill out of sight.

At the end of the Eignor Farm Trail, turn right onto the Colonel Rochester Trail yet again. Right before the junction with the Burroughs Memorial Trail, about 0.1 mile from the end of the red-blazed trail, you will notice a small stone monument tucked about 50 feet off the trail to your left. This tribute, erected in 1921, celebrates the life and works of John Burroughs, a famed nineteenth-century naturalist and essayist, native to the Catskills. His many nature essays speak extensively of the mountains and the wildlife that he held dear.

When you are finished reflecting at the memorial, follow the blue blazes downhill, retracing the way back to your car.

ROCHESTER HOLLOW SHELTER

46

Bearpen and Vly Mountains

DISTANCE: 6.5 miles	
TYPE: Out and back	
TOTAL ELEVATION GAIN: 1,325 feet	
MAXIMUM ELEVATION: 3,600 feet	
DIFFICULTY: Moderate	
HIKING TIME: 3.5 hours	

While being two of the most remote mountains in the region, Bearpen and Vly are included on the list of Catskill peaks above 3,500 feet elevation, at 3,600 feet and 3,529 feet, respectively. What makes these mountains unique, however, is that they are the only high peaks outside the Catskill Park boundary line. In addition, these mountains have no maintained foot trails to their summits. Most untrailed mountains in the Catskills are very strenuous bushwhacks through heavy underbrush and blowdown, but the route up Bearpen and Vly follows broad forest roads, easily discernible herd paths, and snowmobile trails, making for a pleasant hike any time of year. Their far-flung location often affords a good deal of solitude, a highlight not to be overlooked.

GETTING THERE

Take Exit 19 (Kingston) from the New York State Thruway, then turn right onto NY-28, heading west. Continue on NY-28 West for 27 miles until you reach the hamlet of Big Indian. From Big Indian, take NY-28 north for another 5.4 miles, eventually turning right onto Main Street in the small town of Fleischmanns. In half a mile, turn right onto Lake Street/County Route 37. Follow this road for 7.5 miles as it transitions from County Route 37 to Old Halcott Road, and from Old Halcott Road to County Route 3. Parking is available on a gravel pull-off, about a quarter mile from the road's end. The parking area is small but usually not heavily trafficked, due to the secluded location of this hike.

GPS SHORTCUT

Search Google Maps for "Co Rd 3 & Johnson Hollow Road." Follow your GPS

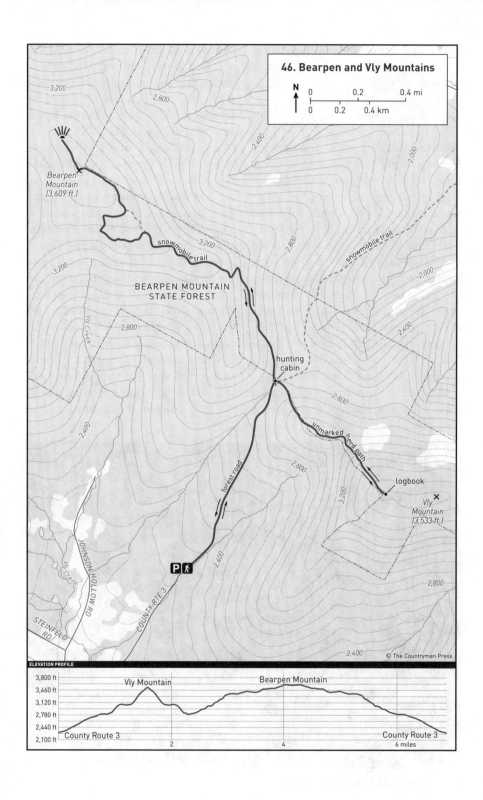

N

| 0 | | 0.2 | | 0.4 mi |
| 0 | 0.2 | | 0.4 km | |

3,200

2,800

2,400

2,000

Bearpen
Mountain
(3,609 ft.)

snowmobile trail

3,200

BEARPEN MOUNTAIN
STATE FOREST

snowmobile trail

2,000

2,800

Vly Creek

2,800

2,400

hunting
cabin

2,800

unmarked herd path

3,200

logbook

Vly ✕
Mountain
(3,533 ft.)

forest road

2,800

JOHNSON HOLLOW RD

Vly Creek

2,800

STEINFELD
RD

COUNTY RTE 3

P 🚶

2,400

2,400

© The Countryman Press

ELEVATION PROFILE

3,800 ft		Vly Mountain		Bearpen Mountain		
3,460 ft						
3,120 ft						
2,780 ft						
2,440 ft						
2,100 ft	County Route 3				County Route 3	

2   4   6 miles

to the intersection and veer right, staying on County Route 3 until your reach the parking area.

THE TRAIL

From the parking area, walk up County Route 3. Enter the woods on a rocky forest road, veering away from a small stream on your right shortly afterward. Climb steadily uphill, following the forest road for roughly a mile until the terrain levels off at about 2,800 feet above sea level. Depending on what season you are hiking, a disused hunting cabin may be visible to your left, along another forest road. This is the saddle between Bearpen and Vly. Continuing straight on will lead you downhill to the other side of the ridge and the continuation of County Route 3.

As the trail levels off, look to your right for some signage marking the boundary of state land. You should be able to discern a well-established herd path a few feet up the trail from these signs. This is the trail to Vly. Leave the forest road and follow this herd path as it winds its way through the trees. There are several short, steep uphill bursts, but for the most part the climb is gradual.

Continue following this herd path until it ends in about three-quarters of a mile. There will be a canister containing a logbook attached to a tree. Sign in if you wish and make your way back to the forest road via the same route you just walked. There is no clear view from the top of Vly, but if the leaves are off the trees, you may catch little glimpses of the surrounding countryside.

Once back at the saddle you can descend back to your vehicle by turning left, or continue to Bearpen by heading toward the hunting cabin,

RUSTY CAR REMNANTS NEAR THE SUMMIT OF BEARPEN MOUNTAIN

LOOKING NORTH FROM BEARPEN MOUNTAIN

following a snowmobile path past a small field. You will come to a trail split shortly thereafter. Stay left and begin to climb uphill. There is a network of unmarked trails and old roads in this area, and it can be confusing to know which trails to take. When in doubt, follow the path that heads uphill! In about 0.3 mile, the trail will switch-back, sending you another 0.2 mile steeply upward. Follow the snowmobile trail for 0.75 mile as it largely levels off. The trail here is easy and gives you plenty of opportunities to look around and take in your surroundings.

Eventually you will begin climbing again along the same snowmobile trail. The path becomes a little rockier at this point. This portion of the trail can be very muddy and slippery when conditions are wet as well. After about half a mile, the trail begins to level off again on a large, flat, wooded plateau. This is the true summit of Bearpen, which, like Vly, does not have any views. Continuing a few hundred feet past the true summit, and downhill a short distance, will bring you to a large clearing that offers very good views of the northern country. Exploring this area further shows evidence of dilapidated man-made structures (probably remnants of ski slopes) and a rusty old car, set a short distance back into the trees.

Once you have finished taking in the view, return to the saddle by the same way you came and walk back down the forest road to your vehicle.

V.

WESTERN

Touch-Me-Not Mountain/ Little Pond/ Cabot Mountain

DISTANCE: 7.5 miles	
TYPE: Lollipop	
TOTAL ELEVATION GAIN: 730 feet	
MAXIMUM ELEVATION: 2,970 feet	
DIFFICULTY: Strenuous	
HIKING TIME: 4.5 hours	

The western section of the Catskill Park is—not surprisingly, simply given its remoteness—far less trafficked than other areas that boast taller mountains and more trail space, but the solitude you'll experience here is absolutely one of the region's highlights. The lightly travelled 584-mile Finger Lakes Trail meanders through the region, traversing some of the more prominent hills and mountains, featuring several vistas from which to view the expansive countryside below. The hike described here takes you to two of these viewpoints and over two of the taller mountains in the Delaware Wild Forest system. While certainly busier than the rest of the trail, the segment following the stream feeding into Little Pond rewards hikers with a look at the history of the area.

GETTING THERE

Follow NY-17 northwest, taking Exit 96 toward Livingston Manor. Turn right onto Debruce Road, and follow it for half a mile. Turn right onto Old Route 17, and then veer right onto Beaverkill Road in 1.3 miles. Follow Beaverkill Road for 8.8 miles before turning left onto Beech Hill Road. The parking area will be on the right, on the edge of a field in about 2.5 miles.

GPS SHORTCUT

Set your GPS to "2282 Beech Hill Road, Andes, NY" and your GPS will navigate you to the appropriate trailhead.

THE TRAIL

From the parking area, head east along a grassy road toward the edge of the woods. You should pick up the red-

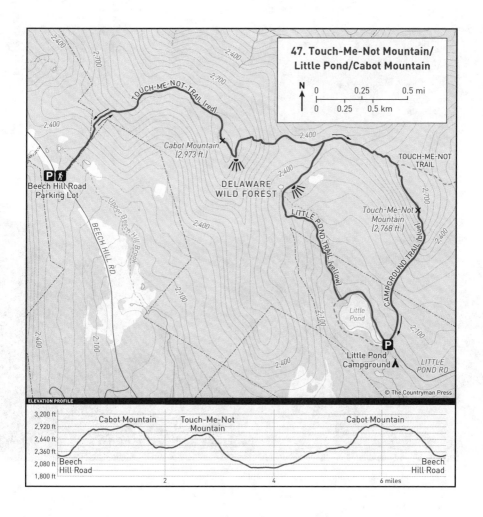

47. Touch-Me-Not Mountain/
Little Pond/Cabot Mountain

N

| 0 | 0.25 | 0.5 mi |
| 0 | 0.25 | 0.5 km |

TOUCH-ME-NOT-TRAIL (red)

Cabot Mountain
(2,973 ft.)

TOUCH-ME-NOT
TRAIL

DELAWARE
WILD FOREST

Beech Hill Road
Parking Lot

Touch-Me-Not
Mountain
(2,768 ft.)

LITTLE POND TRAIL (yellow)

CAMPGROUND TRAIL (blue)

Upper Beech Hill Brook

BEECH HILL RD

Little
Pond

Little Pond
Campground

LITTLE
POND RD

© The Countryman Press

ELEVATION PROFILE

3,200 ft	Cabot Mountain	Touch-Me-Not Mountain	Cabot Mountain	
2,920 ft				
2,640 ft				
2,360 ft				
2,080 ft	Beech Hill Road			Beech Hill Road
1,800 ft		2	4	6 miles

blazed Touch-Me-Not Trail. The Finger Lakes Trail follows this grade across the entire ridge. The trail can be tricky at this point, as there are several boulders and a number of roots that threaten to trip inattentive hikers. After about a quarter of a mile, begin walking steeply uphill on a leafy dirt path. You'll ascend about 650 feet over the course of the next half mile, after which the trail begins to level off significantly. In 1.3 miles from the trailhead, reach the summit of Cabot Mountain, which offers good views looking south from a stone ledge. You'll be able to catch sight of Little Pond in the distance below even when the foliage is thick.

Continue to follow the red blazes heading east. You'll begin to lose elevation shortly, winding through some interesting rock formations. In 0.8 mile the yellow-blazed Little Pond Trail will meet with the Finger Lakes Trail on the right. Stay on the red-blazed trail. This is the col between Cabot Mountain and the shoulder of Touch-Me-Not Mountain. The trail here levels for a short distance before beginning to climb roughly 300 feet, although much less steep than the ascent up Cabot.

LITTLE POND FROM THE VIEWPOINT ON CABOT MOUNTAIN

In 0.4 miles you'll reach the junction of the Campground Trail, a well-defined blue-blazed trail coming in on the right. Turn here and follow the trail onto the relatively narrow summit of Touch-Me-Not Mountain. The hillside to your right drops off fairly quickly, and depending on the foliage, you may be able to catch a view of the pond or Cabot Mountain through the trees. Over the next mile, begin descending until you come to the southern tip of Little Pond. There is a parking area here, as well as several picnic tables.

Stay on the right side of the pond,

following a wide, flat gravel path. This is the southern terminus of the Little Pond Trail. Again, the markers for this trail are yellow, and although they may be somewhat scarce around the pond, the trail is extremely easy to follow. As you walk, you will pass a good number of campsites available for rent along the shoreline, many of them equipped with bear boxes. After about a quarter of a mile, reach a stream feeding into Little Pond and turn right. You will head uphill on a fairly easy grade, passing through sparse tree stands. As you continue, the tree cover will gradually begin to thicken overhead. In a little more than half a mile, an old forest road will meet up with the yellow-blazed trail, coming in on your left. Veer right and join the road grade, continuing to follow the yellow blazes. The canopy opens up as you enter into a grassy meadow, which contains a small weedy pond and the ruins of an old farm. A little further on, there are excellent, wide views to the southeast. There is a lot to take in here, so be sure to set some time aside to explore the area.

When you are ready, reenter the woods on the other side of the meadow, gradually climbing, and rejoin the Finger Lakes Trail in a quarter of a mile. Turn left and head back up and over Cabot Mountain, and down the other side by the way you came, to return to your vehicle.

PANORAMIC VIEW ABOVE LITTLE POND STATE CAMPGROUND

Split Rock Lookout

DISTANCE: 2.4 miles	
TYPE: Out and back	
TOTAL ELEVATION GAIN: 460 feet	
MAXIMUM ELEVATION: 2,670 feet	
DIFFICULTY: Moderate	
HIKING TIME: 2 hours	

Part of the Finger Lakes Trail system in the Delaware Wild Forest, the hike to Split Rock Lookout climbs less than 500 feet, making it a good option for families with children, or those simply seeking a good payoff without too much effort. The vista is often overlooked in favor of bigger ascents and more condensed views to the east, so you'll likely have the view to yourself. There are several options for lengthening your hike, should you wish to do so. Beaverkill, Little Pond, Roscoe, and Miller Hollow campgrounds are all within a half-hour drive of the trailhead, giving you the opportunity to string together a number of hikes throughout the area over the course of a weekend or more.

GETTING THERE

Drive on NY-17 toward Roscoe and take Exit 94. Follow Old Route 17 for half a mile, at which point it becomes NY-206 West. Continue to follow NY-206 for 2.5 miles and turn right onto Beaverkill Valley Road. When you come to a bridge crossing the Beaver Kill, stay left and continue on. Beaverkill Valley Road becomes Berry Brook Road 1.2 miles after passing the bridge. Drive on Berry Brook Road, winding uphill for 4.2 miles. The parking area is a grassy turn-off near the top of the ridge on the right side of the road.

GPS SHORTCUT

Instruct your GPS to navigate you to the intersection of Holiday Brook Road & Berry Brook Road, Roscoe, NY, only a short distance from where the trail starts.

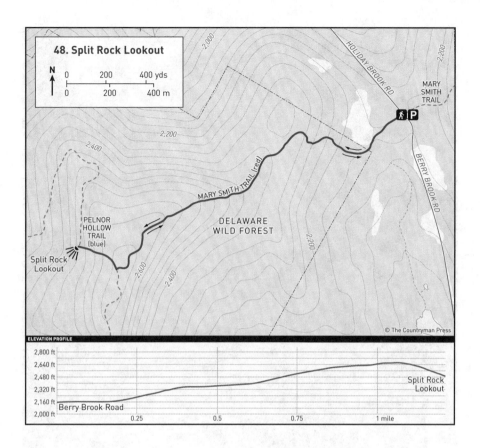

ELEVATION PROFILE

THE TRAIL

Sign in at the trail register located at the northern end of the parking area. Pick up the main trail grade, which edges a hayfield to the left and slightly behind the register. Cross the road and continue into the forest on the red-blazed Mary Smith Trail, which sits to the left of a private driveway. (The Finger Lakes Trail also shares these paths for the entirety of this hike.) The first portion of this hike crosses private land, so be respectful of the landowner's rights and do not stray from the marked trail.

In a few hundred feet, you will come to a power line swath. Go straight across it, and reenter the woods just

below an old stone fence. The trail will climb slightly as you reach the boundary of the state-owned Delaware Wild Forest. Continue to hike on this rarely used footpath, and pass a large rock formation to your right in a short distance. There is a burst of steep climbing immediately after this ledge, bending to the right, along a narrow brushy length of trail, but the incline mellows afterward.

As you ascend, the trail will become rockier, often passing small boulders slightly off-trail, but it is well marked and still quite easy to walk. Your route will level out and resume climbing gradually several times until you reach the top of the ridge. The forest

THE MEANDERING TRAIL TO SPLIT ROCK LOOKOUT

here is dark and densely wooded, mostly comprising maple and beech trees, but you will start to see some oak trees as you progress.

After you hike for 1.2 miles, the Mary Smith Trail ends at the junction of the blue-blazed Pelnor Hollow Trail. When you come to this intersection, turn right and begin heading downhill. Turning left here will take you to the Pelnor Hollow Shelter in 2.2 miles. Oak will become much more dominant on this side of the hill, and you will pass several very large, uniquely eroded boulders as you descend. After dropping roughly 150 feet over the course of 0.2 mile, you will come to a sign marking the obvious viewing area, a small grassy clearing next to an exposed rock face. There is a slabby boulder teetering on the edge of a crack that is about 10 feet deep, where it appears that the rock face has split from the grassy area, the attribute that gives this lookout its name. The vista faces southwest, looking out over the Beaverkill Valley and

THE MARY SMITH TRAIL TO THE JUNCTION OF THE PELNOR HOLLOW TRAIL

VIEW FROM SPLIT ROCK LOOKOUT

other areas of the Delaware Wild Forest system.

When you are ready to leave, turn around and make the steep climb uphill back to the trail junction and follow the red-blazed Mary Smith Trail back to your vehicle. Alternatively, you could lengthen your hike by staying on the Pelnor Hollow Trail, which continues on another mile from the lookout before intersecting with the yellow-blazed Little Spring Brook Trail, which veers south, and the northwest-leading Campbell Mountain Trail, which is also blazed blue.

49

Andes Rail Trail and Bullet Hole Spur

DISTANCE: 3.9 miles	
TYPE: Lollipop	
TOTAL ELEVATION GAIN: 160 feet	
MAXIMUM ELEVATION: 1,840 feet	
DIFFICULTY: Easy	
HIKING TIME: 2 hours	

Although it is roughly 6 miles outside the boundary of the Catskill Park, the Andes Rail Trail offers hikers scenic views of the Tremperskill Valley, as well as interesting historic facts pertaining to the railroad itself. The trail was built as a collaborative effort between Andes Works! and the Catskill Mountain Club, and it is very well maintained. The first mile of the hike follows the railroad grade and is flat and easy, suitable for hikers of all ages. The spur is more strenuous, but it is well worth the effort, as it allows you to experience quiet forest in a memorable setting.

GETTING THERE

From the New York State Thruway, follow NY-28 West for approximately 57 miles. You will pass by Arkville and Margaretville before NY-28 starts heading north, leaving the Catskill Park and then bending to the west. Continue to follow the road to the village of Andes. Go straight onto Depot Street in downtown Andes, leaving NY-28 as it turns to the right and heads due north. The trailhead is well marked and will be on your left, 0.3 mile after you leave NY-28. Park on the wide gravel shoulder just above the trailhead.

GPS SHORTCUT

Direct your GPS to navigate you to the town of Andes, NY, then follow the above instructions.

THE TRAIL

Walk through a wooden gate bearing the Andes Rail Trail sign and pass a long, white building. This is the Depot Building, which was erected in 1907. Originally this was a stop on the rail-

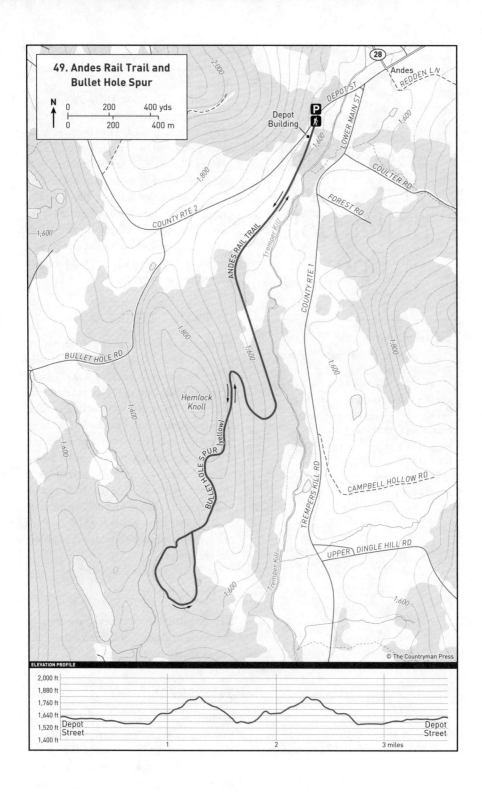

49. Andes Rail Trail and Bullet Hole Spur

N

| 0 | 200 | 400 yds |
| 0 | 200 | 400 m |

Andes
REDDEN LN
28
DEPOT ST
Depot Building
LOWER MAIN ST
COULTER RD
FOREST RD
COUNTY RTE 2
Tremper Kill
COUNTY RTE 1
ANDES RAIL TRAIL
1,800
1,600
2,000
BULLET HOLE RD
1,800
Hemlock Knoll
BULLET HOLE SPUR (yellow)
1,600
CAMPBELL HOLLOW RD
TREMPERS KILL RD
Tremper Kill
UPPER DINGLE HILL RD
1,600
1,600

© The Countryman Press

ELEVATION PROFILE

2,000 ft				
1,880 ft				
1,760 ft				
1,640 ft				
1,520 ft	Depot Street			Depot Street
1,400 ft				
	1	2	3 miles	

FOOTBRIDGE OVER A MUDDY SEGMENT OF THE RAIL TRAIL

road that served the town of Andes. The building was abandoned in 1924, but it has recently been restored.

After passing the Depot Building, pick up the railroad grade as it enters the woods. There will be a trail register on your right, so be sure to sign in. Continue on the railroad grade, which is unmarked but easy to follow. You'll pass over a wet area on a small footbridge shortly after you sign in. The land on either side of the trail is privately owned, so stay on the path. As you walk, you'll periodically come to signs offering interesting facts about the history of the railroad and the area itself. At certain points you will notice small bits of coal still littering the trail. For the most part, the grade is flat and grassy, but it may be slightly bumpy at times, due to the

SIGNAGE MARKING THE START OF THE ANDES RAIL TRAIL

railroad ties that are still buried beneath the trail.

Pass through an open field offering bucolic views of the adjacent hillsides. There are the remnants of a turntable used to move locomotives about halfway through the field on your right. Reenter the woods, crossing a small bridge, and shortly thereafter you will have a second chance to take in the countryside, this time from a clearing along a trail detour. The detour parallels the rail trail and is intended to be used when the main trail is muddy. There is another mud detour

a little further on as well. In the valley below, you can see the lazy Tremper Kill and the beaver dams that have altered its course.

After 1 mile, the rail trail ends, and the spur segment begins. The spur is blazed with yellow square markers and turns immediately to the right, heading uphill moderately. Follow the blazes as the trail makes its way uphill, switching back a few times. You'll ascend up and around the hillside, passing several rock formations in a stand of old hemlock trees. The trail turns to the left and begins a short descent into open forest shortly after this. When you come to a stone fence on the edge of a field, turn right and walk alongside the field, following the markers. In a few hundred feet, you'll turn left, passing through a small notch in the fence. The trail splits shortly thereafter at the corner of a pine grove. This is the start of the loop portion of the trail.

Turn right here and descend slightly along the edge of the pines. Continu-ing to follow the yellow markers, you will enter a dark hemlock forest. The trail curves to the left, crossing another stone wall and ascending to the edge of the pine grove again. Follow the trail as it skirts around the pine trees and eventually returns to the start of the loop.

To return to your car, follow the yellow blazes back to the rail trail, and walk the railroad grade back to the parking area.

LOOKING OUT OVER THE TREMPER KILL

50

Trout Pond Loop

DISTANCE: 5.1 miles	
TYPE: Loop	
TOTAL ELEVATION GAIN: 760 feet	
MAXIMUM ELEVATION: 2,475 feet	
DIFFICULTY: Easy	
HIKING TIME: 2.5 hours	

A popular destination for fishing, the Trout Pond loop also has several highlights to attract hikers looking for an easy walk through quiet woods. The route follows wide snowmobile trails, climbing less than 1,000 feet, and visits two scenic ponds that offer swimming, camping, and fishing. Additionally, you can see the ruins of a few settlements, and a very pretty waterfall. There are several primitive campsites on the drive down to the trailhead, as well as two shelters and half a dozen campsites around the pond itself, making this an excellent choice for explorers seeking a relaxing weekend getaway. Do note that all swimming should be done at your own risk.

GETTING THERE

Drive on NY-17 toward Roscoe and take Exit 94. Follow Old Route 17 north for half a mile, at which point it becomes NY-206 West. Follow NY-206 for 2 miles and turn left onto Morton Hill Road. Stay on Morton Hill Road for 3 miles. Turn left onto Russell Brook Road and follow it downhill for about a mile, until you come to a parking area marked by a large trail sign. There are several places to pull off and camp as you make your way down. This road is seasonal and is not maintained from December to April. Even when it is maintained, it is rocky and often uneven, so proceed with caution.

GPS SHORTCUT

Type "Mud Pond & Trout Pond Hiking Trail and Campgrounds" into Google Maps to have your GPS navigate you to the appropriate trailhead.

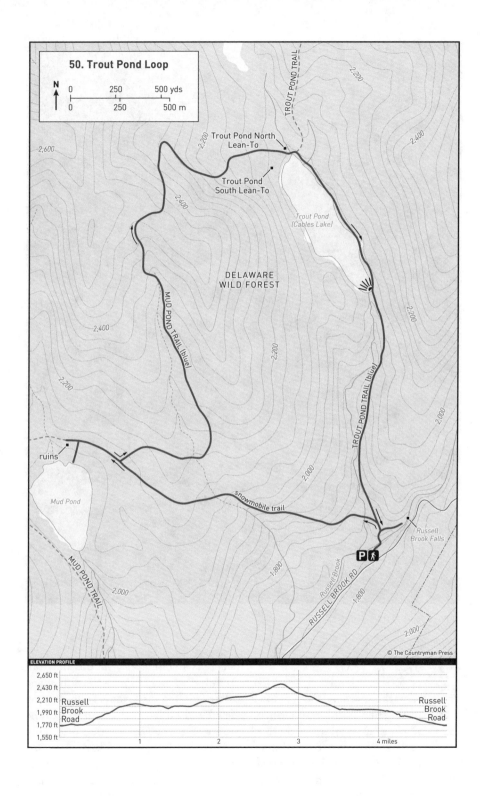

50. Trout Pond Loop

N

| 0 | 250 | 500 yds |
| 0 | 250 | 500 m |

2,200

TROUT POND TRAIL

2,200

2,400

2,600

2,200

Trout Pond North
Lean-To

Trout Pond
South Lean-To

2,400

Trout Pond
(Cables Lake)

DELAWARE
WILD FOREST

2,400

2,400

2,200

MUD POND TRAIL (blue)

2,200

2,200

2,000

TROUT POND TRAIL (blue)

2,000

ruins

Mud Pond

snowmobile trail

2,000

Russell
Brook Falls

1,800

P

MUD POND TRAIL

RUSSELL BROOK RD

2,000

1,800

Russell Brook

2,000

© The Countryman Press

ELEVATION PROFILE

| 2,650 ft |
| 2,430 ft |
| 2,210 ft | Russell
| 1,990 ft | Brook
| 1,770 ft | Road
| 1,550 ft |

Russell
Brook
Road

1   2   3   4 miles

RUSSELL BROOK FALLS

THE TRAIL

From the parking area, descend down a well-established trail on an old jeep road, following it for about a tenth of a mile. You will cross a bridge spanning Russell Brook, and make your way around a small grove of old apple trees.

There is an unmarked but obvious trail running off to the right a short distance after crossing the bridge. Following it a few hundred feet will bring you to the ruins of a stone bridge that originally ran across Russell Brook. A little further upstream you can see Russell Brook Falls, a very pretty waterfall that stands about 40 feet tall. If the water level is high, it may be difficult to reach the foot of the falls without getting wet. When you are finished exploring here, return to the road grade to continue your hike.

A short distance from the trail to the falls, arrive at a trail register, just before the trail splits. Sign in and go left at the fork, heading up a wide, blue-blazed snowmobile trail that climbs gradually, ascending about 300 feet over the course of half a mile. The terrain is easy here, giving you the opportunity to look around and take in the scenery as you walk.

A mile from the trail split, you will reach the junction of the Mud Pond Trail, which is also blazed blue. You will eventually want to turn here and follow the trail uphill, but for now go straight. Mud Pond is visible through the trees off to your left, and in 0.2 mile you will pass a large campsite, which sits below a very old maple tree. A wide herd path next to the tree will lead you down to the water's edge. A little farther up the main trail, you can see the decaying bluestone foundations of a previous settlement dotting the woods. Another campsite lies beyond the last foundation, a short distance from the shore.

Return to the trail juncture and turn left to follow the blue markers uphill on a grassy trail that crosses over an old stone fence shortly thereafter. The trail is a little rockier after passing this fence, but it is still quite easy. You will climb

NEAR THE NORTHERN END OF TROUT POND

TRAIL SIGNS MARKING THE START OF THE LOOP

moderately, slightly more than before, for about a mile. Once you crest the hill, the trail veers to the right and begins descending. The descent is steeper than the climb, and drops about 450 feet over the course of a mile, although the trail is less rocky and wider than it was for the duration of the ascent.

Toward the end of the Mud Pond Trail, you will come to the northern tip of Trout Pond. There are good views looking out over the water from here, as well as two shelters, and a number of primitive campsites scattered all around the pond. Follow the trail as it passes the northernmost shelter, and cross a series of wide bridges over small inlet streams that feed the pond. Immediately after passing the shelter,

you will notice the continuation of the Trout Pond Trail to your left, heading north. Ignore this split, and follow the trail south, along the side of the water on a flat, grassy snowmobile trail. At the southern tip of Trout Pond, there is a large gravelly clearing next to a concrete spillway, which provides nicer, more open views looking back up the water. This would be a nice place to go for a swim.

Continue to follow the snowmobile path as it heads downhill, passing a few hemlock stands. The trail will gradually drop roughly 200 feet, and in 0.75 mile, you will reach the junction where you started and the trail register. From here, sign out and make the short trek back to your car.

Index

Italics indicates maps and illustrations.